AUDI QUATTRO
Rally Car

1980 to 1987 (includes Group 4 & Group B rally cars)

First published in August 2019

A catalogue record for this book is available from the British Library.

ISBN 978 1 78521 250 5

Library of Congress control no. 2019934669

Published by Haynes Publishing,
Sparkford, Yeovil, Somerset BA22 7JJ, UK.
Tel: 01963 440635
Int. tel: +44 1963 440635
Website: www.haynes.com

Haynes North America Inc.,
859 Lawrence Drive, Newbury Park,
California 91320, USA.

Printed in Malaysia.

AUDI QUATTRO
Rally Car

1980 to 1987 (includes Group 4 & Group B rally cars)

Enthusiasts' Manual

An insight into the design, engineering and competition
history of Audi's iconic rally car

Nick Garton

Contents

OPPOSITE **The Audi Quattro redefined rally cars and put Audi on the top table of the automotive world.** (*Audi AG*)

Introduction

When I have told people the subject of my latest outing for Haynes, one response has been offered long before any other: 'Fire up the Quattro!' That's because to most people these days, at least in the English-speaking world, the first association that springs to mind with Audi's groundbreaking, brand-defining coupé is the catchphrase of a slightly thuggish comedy throwback copper, DCI Gene Hunt. Hunt existed in a fictional Thatcherite London but was played with such bravado by actor Philip Glenister that he – and his Tornado Red-painted Quattro – have attained iconic status.

But why was the Quattro chosen as the ultimate emblem of the 1980s? Glenister himself had the answer: 'As a child I would spend hours watching rallying on Saturday mornings and it was always the Quattro – usually in red and white or a rather strange orange colour – that would be tearing up the field... Everyone agreed: the Audi Quattro would be perfect.'

Not that the real-life Quattro was without

a catchphrase of its own – in this case, the infinitely subtler *Vorsprung durch Technik*. The phrase was 'borrowed' from a faded workshop poster by advertising legend Sir John Hegarty and has endured as Audi's brand strapline to this day. It has survived pop culture encounters from the likes of Blur and U2 but never sounded better than when drawled lugubriously by Geoffrey Palmer over Audi's TV adverts of the day.

Today, the word quattro (with a small 'q') remains the pinnacle of Audi's engineering achievements, whether attached to world-beating touring cars, Le Mans-winning sports cars, sleek executive expresses or imposing SUVs. But it is in rallying that the Quattro set the tone for a story that has lasted for 40 years.

I should like to dedicate this book to the memory of Rodney Clinch, company secretary of VAG in Britain throughout the Quattro's rallying years and father of one of my dearest childhood friends. Early in 1982, Rodney took three small boys out in the petrol blue press car that *Autocar* had covered 12,000 miles in… and its pace around the lanes of Northamptonshire leaves us dumbfounded to this day.

LEFT TV detective **Gene Hunt introduced the Quattro to a new generation in the BBC drama** *Ashes to Ashes. (REX/ Shutterstock)*

Acknowledgements

My most grateful thanks to so many people for bringing this book to life: Allan Durham at Pro-Tec Motorsport, Andy Dawson and Dawson Auto Developments, Fred Gallagher, Michèle Mouton, John Buffum, Malcolm Wilson, Phil Short, Satwant Singh Ghataure, Ari Vatanen, Sarel van der Merwe, David Ingram and Reinhard Klein who were in the thick of the action. Also to Adam Marsden at AM Quattro, Darron Edwards, Nick Barrington, Bob Dennis, John Polson and the Bonhams team, Mark Donaldson, Kari Mäkelä and Jari-Matti Latvala for their knowledge and expertise on the cars today.

Enormous gratitude is also due to the many contributors whose work appears in this book. To Lucy Bamber, daughter of the late, great motor sport artist Jim Bamber, and to her mother, who allowed us to use Jim's peerless cutaway artwork. To everyone at McKlein for their expertise and extensive archive and the archives of *Motor Sport* magazine. To Franz

Lang and the IG-Audi Sport veterans for endless fact-checking (all mistakes my own!), Martin Holmes, for wisdom and images and the members of Facebook groups such as Audi Quattro UK, the Audi Quattro Owners' Club, Group B Today and Group B Rally Legends.

More thanks still to Martyn Pass, Audi's motor sport PR Svengali, Peter Kober at Audi Tradition, to the press office at Bosch, Tobias Mauler at Porsche AG and Tanya Dempsey at Kudos. To Tim Foster and Rallying With Group B, to the Slowly Sideways community, the Audi Quattro Owners' Club, Jonathan Gill and MPA Media, Richard Rodgers, Judy and Richard Southwell, Jeremy Walton, Stephen Wright and Staffs Slot Cars, Gareth Jex, Janet Garton, Andrea Seed at Poppyseed Media, Guy Clinch, Kaj Lindberg, Richard Armon, Callum Pudge, Paul Judson, Gary Walton and Lawrence Clift for helping to make this book as good as it can be.

And finally, thanks once again to Steve Rendle and all at Haynes for the opportunity to tell this story, and to my wife and family for tolerating my frequent absences to pursue glorious old rally cars.

Chapter One

The Audi Quattro story

Although the Audi Quattro revolutionised rallying, it's hard to point to any single aspect of its design or construction and say that it was groundbreaking. What the engineers behind the Quattro brought to the sport of rallying, and as a result to the wider automotive world, was the combination and refinement of these technologies in a truly virtuoso manner.

OPPOSITE The Audi Quattro was the embodiment of one man's determination to haul a half-forgotten brand to the top of Germany's motor industry. That man was Ferdinand Piëch. *(McKlein)*

In this can be seen the hand of the man who was the guiding light of Audi engineering: Ferdinand Karl Piëch, who was instrumental in bringing the programme to life. Only recently, a senior Volkswagen executive said of Piëch: 'He was a great man for solving problems with other people's ideas. He knew immediately when he saw a good idea, like Picasso seeing an African mask and making it into art.'

The Quattro was undoubtedly Piëch's finest masterpiece.

Whispers from the north

Poke around most major towns in Germany for five minutes and you will find men and women with extraordinary knowledge about engineering motor cars. The streets are thick with experts on paint, metallurgy, fuel, lubricants, suspension, electronics and how to make doors shut with an almost imperceptible 'clunk'. It has been this way for 100 years.

One such expert, quietly going about his business in Ingolstadt during the mid-1970s, was Jörg Bensinger; a 47-year-old transmission specialist with Audi, the unremarkable large car brand that had recently been attached to Volkswagen.

The transmission needs of Audi's then-current range of cars, consisting of front-wheel-drive 80 and 100 saloons, were not unduly

RIGHT Transmission specialist Jörg Bensinger was the first senior Audi technician to realise the potential of four-wheel drive. *(Audi AG)*

taxing for a man of Bensinger's abilities and so he had been given other responsibilities to take care of. One of these was speaking at seminars and to the motoring press, while the other was developing new transmission systems within the Volkswagen group.

In 1976, Bensinger's presence was required in the snowy wastes of northern Finland, where trials of a new Volkswagen off-road vehicle were being held. A decade earlier, as Europe began the long road towards integration (and prevent potential rogue states like France from backing out), the Merger Treaty brought management of the European Coal and Steel Community, the European Atomic Energy Community and the European Economic Community under one roof. Together, these communities launched a series of collaborative projects between the member nations.

Among these projects, it was decided that the armed forces of Europe needed a new kind of Jeep. The British had their Land Rovers and the Americans were barrelling round in Fords that looked almost identical to their Second World War predecessors, but between Europe's car makers, it was believed an even better solution could be found.

Numerous prototypes of amphibious off-road vehicles were produced by trinities as unlikely as Fiat (Italy), M.A.N. (Germany) and Saviem (France), and that of Hotchkiss (France), Büssing (Germany) and Lancia (Italy), but in the end nobody could agree on anything except that the prototypes were not very good.

Eventually, the German government got bored of wasting money in this way and pulled out of the 'Europa Jeep' idea completely – instead going to Volkswagen with its brief to design an all-terrain vehicle. What came back was the Volkswagen Type 181, an updated version of the wartime *Kübelwagen* (bucket car), which had used Volkswagen Beetle components on a raised chassis with a boxy body on the top.

There was no argument that the Kübelwagen was a great off-road car – in comparison testing during the war, the Allies discovered that the rear-engine, two-wheel-drive German car was superior to the Jeep in most battlefield conditions – but it was somewhat dated. Visually and mechanically the Type 181 was simply a

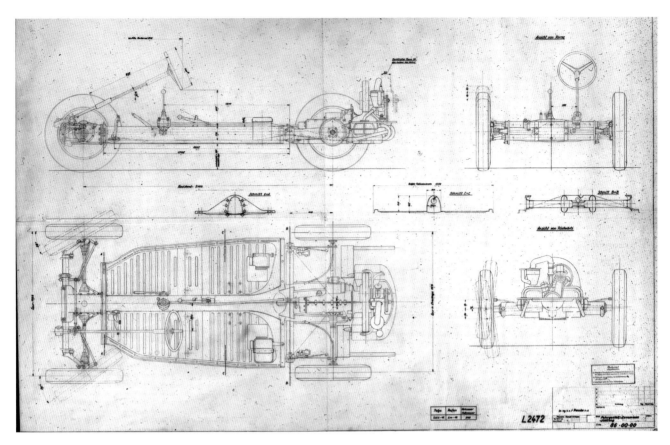

reworking of the car that had conquered Europe in 1940 – and this design was accepted by the government as an interim measure.

Seeking a longer-term solution, Volkswagen looked to Ingolstadt, home of the four Auto Union brands that it had purchased in 1964. Here the VW engineers found the DKW Munga (named after an Estonian monk!) which was a simple, lightweight four-wheel-drive forestry worker's car that had been built from 1956 to 1968. The Munga was fitted with more modern suspension, a new four-wheel-drive system based around components from the Audi 100 and a 1.7-litre, four-cylinder Volkswagen engine producing 75 PS (55 kW).

Jörg Bensinger was asked to test drive the result and called the Volkswagen *Iltis* (polecat), in the Arctic conditions of Finland, in order to give his opinion on its transmission to the development team. Among the engineers most heavily involved with the Iltis was a young member of Bensinger's team who was very excited about the car. His name was Roland Gumpert.

By hooning around the Finnish roads in the Iltis, Gumpert showed Bensinger that putting

ABOVE Ferdinand Porsche's Kübelwagen military vehicle had experimented with four-wheel drive during the Second World War. *(Porsche AG)*

BELOW After pulling out of the 'Europa jeep' initiative, Germany's armed forces were equipped with an updated Kübelwagen that became a popular leisure vehicle. *(Volkswagen AG)*

the power down through all four wheels could make a car – even a narrow, top-heavy brick like this – remarkably sprightly on a normal road. There was a small fleet of Audi 80s on hand and naturally the young engineers had compared their performance to discover that while the Iltis was left for dead by conventional cars on a straight road, it would catch them up in no time on slippery corners.

This was something that Bensinger had been considering for a long time, particularly with regard to tyre wear on regular two-wheel-drive cars. In Britain, Jensen sports cars had built an extravagant GT with four-wheel drive and in Japan, Subaru had introduced the first mass-produced four-wheel-drive passenger car in 1972, the Leone, which was proving to be a big hit in snowy climes.

Bensinger decided to follow up on Gumpert's enthusiasm for four-wheel drive. 'This was very interesting, putting all these things on paper, but we had no possibility to build such a car when I was thinking about such things,' he later remembered.

'I wanted to try 4x4 on better surfaces. When I came back from that winter testing I said to Mr Piëch that we should do this 4x4 for a higher performance car, like a 100. Mr Piëch was not very excited about this, when I told him how good the Iltis had been. But it was only the next morning when he telephones me and we talk about the idea. He says we must convince the public of the advantages of 4x4 and that we can do it at Audi.'

Game of thrones

The vast German automotive industry from which the Audi Quattro emerged has a long history of technical innovation, motor sport success and prestige earned through the quality of its engineering. Yet at its heart lies a tale of conquest and collaboration, alliances and schisms that could rival even the most lavish fictional saga. To understand how the Quattro was created, it is important to have a grasp upon the titanic monster that spawned it.

Motoring was born during 1895 when the engineer Gottlieb Daimler and his partner, William Maybach, had worked away on gasoline-powered internal combustion engines in Cannstatt, a district of Stuttgart. Meanwhile, in nearby Mannheim another engineer, Karl Benz, was also determined to prove that such engines could unleash the great age of adventure on land, water and ultimately in the air.

These were heady days for ambitious engineers and soon motor manufacturers began to spring up across Europe. One among them was founded in 1896 by an engineer from Daimler's own factory; a man named August Horch.

Horch chose Saxony for his headquarters, attracting local investment from the region to establish a factory in the town of Chemnitz.

His luxurious and smooth-running cars gained an enviable reputation, upon which Horch very swiftly sold shares in the company. Then after a disagreement with his financial officer in 1909, August Horch was ousted from the company by his shareholders and forced to start all over again.

A legal battle cost Horch the use of his own name, which would remain registered to the company from which he had just been ejected, and so a suitable replacement needed to be found. 'Horch' is a form of the German verb to harken, so he and his investors chose Audi, the same word from the Latin language.

As with so many motor manufacturers of the age, the nascent Audi chose motor sport as a means to promote its new products. Competitions from hill climbs to grand prix racing had become a European obsession in which cars wore national racing colours and the white cars of the Kaiser's Germany conquered all.

Chief among them was Mercedes, the brand name chosen for Daimler's passenger cars, which gained iconic status as a grand prix winner. Technical brilliance was a priority of the Kaiser's Germany, and armadas of white-painted racing cars were sent out while German dreadnoughts thundered down the slipways and Graf Zeppelin's airships dominated the sky.

Soon, however, all of this industry would be harnessed to the Great War of 1914–18. The

LEFT Horch chose to establish his own factory in eastern Germany but was forced out of Daimler in 1909. *(Audi AG)*

motor manufacturers of Germany and Austria-Hungary switched production to service vast military contracts until the guns fell silent in 1918, when Germany's defeat brought chaos and long, bleak years of privation.

If Karl Benz, Gottlieb Daimler and Wilhelm Maybach should share credit for creating the motor car, it was Dr Emil Georg von Stauß who, in his role on the board of Deutsche Bank, effectively founded the modern German automotive industry. It was von Stauß who sought to impose economies of scale upon Daimler and Benz, leading to their merger in 1926 and the resulting brand of Mercedes-Benz.

BELOW LEFT Horch and his investors were barred from claiming the Horch name, so settled upon the Latin equivalent: Audi. *(Audi AG)*

BELOW August Horch was enthusiastic about motor sport, seen here at the wheel of the 1908 Horch Torpedo, resplendent in German racing white. *(Audi AG)*

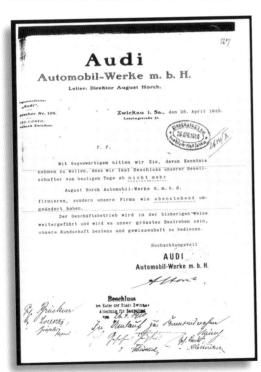

RIGHT In the barren economic climate of the 1920s, Emil Georg von Stauß brought Mercedes and Benz together as a single entity. *(Daimler AG)*

BELOW The Sindelfingen factory not only built Mercedes-Benz products but also the first BMW road cars and the VW Beetle prototypes. *(Daimler AG)*

Into this partnership, von Stauß later introduced another of Deutsche Bank's creditors, the Bayerische Motoren Werke (BMW), from Munich. Under a new 'Treaty of Friendship', BMW and Daimler-Benz exchanged shareholdings and a licensed copy of Britain's little Austin 7, dubbed the BMW 3/15, went into production at Daimler's Sindelfingen plant – founding what became known as 'Deutschland AG' (Germany plc).

While von Stauß laboured over his investments, in Frankfurt the Opel factory was completely restructured along American lines and began to churn out cheap cars that soon would account for 40% of all German production. At that point the American giant, General Motors, swept in to buy Opel outright, threatening to derail von Stauß's dream of cherry-picking the brands he needed to create a single German entity for car production.

Where General Motors went, its great American rival Ford swiftly followed: opening a factory of its own in Cologne. German research in America revealed that it took a company like Mercedes 50 times the number of man-hours to produce a single car than Ford, but before production could be modernised the tsunami of the Great Depression arrived.

The 'Treaty of Friendship' helped Deutsche Bank's factories to weather the storm but in Saxony the factories of Horch, Audi, DKW and Wanderer were foundering. All seemed lost until, at the last minute, the regional assembly of Saxony decided to invest in its own collective; creating a single new entity called Auto Union with the emblem of four rings representing its founding brands.

Within a year, Germany had adopted the totalitarian rule of National Socialism to find a way out of impoverishment. It helped the motor manufacturers that Adolf Hitler was a car buff and that one of his dearest-held ambitions was for all of Germany to be put on wheels. For all the trumpeting of its technological wonders, Germany could only boast of one car per hundred

LEFT Marshalling the finances of the Third Reich and making the German automotive industry ever-more powerful were the preoccupations of von Stauß, fourth from right. *(Getty Images)*

inhabitants, compared to three for every hundred British or French citizens and one car for every five Americans. This was an intolerable affront to German supremacy, in Hitler's view.

The Führer decreed that Germany would return to international motor sport and dominate as it had before the Great War, showcasing the technical mastery of the new Reich. There would be fast, wide autobahns upon which to mobilise *dem Deutschen volke* and a boom in car sales for domestic manufacturers. What he lacked was a truly affordable car for even the most modest of households.

Even before Hitler was in power, the astute Dr Emil Georg von Stauß had positioned himself as the Führer's banker and his right-hand man on motoring matters. He shared Hitler's vision of motorising German society and he knew exactly the man to bring this vision to life. That man was the brilliant but difficult former Mercedes designer, Ferdinand Porsche.

Porsche's brilliance as an engineer was first demonstrated in 1899, when he built a revolutionary 'horseless carriage' for Jacob Lohner & Company, celebrated Viennese coachbuilder to the royal families of Europe. Using a motor of his own design, Porsche's electric car could travel 50 miles (80km) on a single charge and reach 22mph (35kph) – faster than most contemporary gasoline and steam cars.

When customers demanded even more speed and range he developed the world's first gasoline-electric hybrid car: the Lohner-Porsche Mixte Hybrid. It was important to note the new car's hyphenated name, because while Porsche's thirst for engineering was vast, it was rivalled by his desire for fame and fortune.

Lohner's clientele brought Porsche into the circles of power but its horizons were limited. In 1906 he joined the Austrian offshoot of Daimler as head of design, overseeing a cornucopia of luxurious cars, heavyweight trucks, buses, ships and trains, all powered by internal combustion engines. During the First World War, Porsche's role saw him design arguably the best aero engine of the war, the straight-six Austro-Daimler. He also witnessed the enormous benefits – and profits – that could be wrung from mass production.

After the war, Porsche relocated to Stuttgart and the heart of Daimler-Benz, where he designed a series of racing cars to showcase Mercedes technology that was crowned with the supercharged SSK. Their victories brought Porsche more renown but as early as 1926, Porsche was agitating to push ahead with the idea of a small, cheap car to be sold to the masses. Daimler-Benz eventually turned him down and so Porsche chose to leave.

He briefly returned to Austria with Steyr but again the idea of a *Volks-wagen* (people's car) was rejected and he walked away from that job, too. Through these travails, von Stauß had maintained personal links with Porsche and in 1931 counselled him to set up an independent design bureau. With Porsche's son-in-law Anton Piëch managing the legal and administrative side of the agency, the capital to get the Porsche Design Bureau underway was raised by another of von Stauß's contacts, the wealthy former Benz racing driver, Alfred Rosenberger.

BELOW Young genius Ferdinand Porsche sits alongside the driver of a Lohner-Porsche hybrid motor car in 1901. *(Porsche AG)*

BOTTOM In 1933, von Stauß arranged for a meeting between Porsche, Auto Union and Adolf Hitler to agree the finances of a revolutionary rear-engined grand prix car. *(Audi AG)*

Porsche's agency started out by designing a simple mid-range car for Wanderer, while trying and failing to get Porsche's low-cost *Volks-wagen* concept off the ground with DKW and motorcycle manufacturer NSU. Their next big project was for a grand prix racing car that would be funded by Auto Union and the German government.

The Auto Union project got Porsche in front of Hitler himself, where finally the great designer found himself with a receptive audience for his plan to make motoring affordable for all. In time, Hitler duly claimed all the credit and renamed the *Volks-wagen* as the less catchy *Kraft durch Freude-wagen (KdF-wagen)* (strength through joy car, representing the government department for leisure and the workforce).

For his part, von Stauß put in place the management structure for this vast project, with representatives of BMW, Daimler-Benz, Auto Union, Opel and others all sitting in on the

planning commission – truly, 'Deutschland AG' was out in full force.

Hitler laid the foundations of a new factory at the Saxon village of Fallersleben, and while the factory was under construction Porsche's prototype *KdF-wagens* were built at Mercedes' Sindelfingen plant. Then, just as the project was about to reach fruition, the Second World War happened – and ultimately another, altogether more crushing defeat for Germany.

After the war, the site at Fallersleben was among the first of Germany's bomb-blasted factories to splutter back into life. Originally, the plan had been for the British occupying army to dismantle the factory and ship it back for one of its domestic motor manufacturers to use – but nobody in Britain believed that the car was viable. Neither did the Americans, which meant that the factory was handed back to the Germans, who renamed Fallersleben as the Volkswagenwerk and employed former Opel boss Heinz Nordhoff to manage operations.

A phenomenal success resulted. In total, 21,529,464 of Porsche's air-cooled utility vehicles were built through 65 years of production, turning Volkswagen into a global automotive powerhouse – making the Porsche family a fortune. Anton Piëch had taken 10 million Reichmarks out of Volkswagen in 1945 to establish Porsche as a manufacturer of Volkswagen-based sports cars, based initially at its wartime satellite works in Gmünd, Austria.

After the war, Ferdinand Porsche was arrested for war crimes as a result of lobbying by the senior management of Peugeot. No verifiable charges were brought, but it was true that many of the labourers on Porsche's wartime projects (as the head of weapons development) had been transported from Peugeot's factories in occupied France. Many of them had been mistreated and a number of them had died.

Effectively, the aged Ferdinand Porsche was held to ransom and so Ferry Porsche and Anton Piëch had taken on an array of clients to help fund their patriarch's release. Most notable among them was a magnificent grand prix car, the Cisitalia 360, which featured four-wheel drive among its many innovations.

The family set up a Volkswagen dealership in Salzburg to be run by Louise Piëch and Ferry

Porsche began constructing a Volkswagen-based sports car, which would become known as the Porsche 356. Soon the firm would move back into the rubble-strewn ruins of Germany, in Stuttgart-Zuffenhausen, as the rest of the Fatherland's automotive industry was slowly coming back to life.

Emil Georg von Stauß had died in 1942 but the collaboration that he had fostered was not buried with him. Deutsche Bank was still heavily invested and so too was the Quandt family, who owned 10% of Daimler and 30% of BMW. In the 1950s the idea was tabled that the Bavarian operation should simply be swallowed up by Daimler but friction among the shareholders saw the Quandts save BMW from extinction by funding the Neue Klasse (new class) series of small but powerful executive cars, and eventually they sold their stake in Daimler to the Kuwaiti royal family.

All was less solvent in Saxony, home of Audi and the other components of Auto Union. The region was overrun by the Red Army in 1945 and, in the great partition of East and West Germany, the management and much of the workforce made a break to the West before the Iron Curtain fell. They established a new Auto Union company in Ingolstadt, building pre-war DKW designs.

These cars had little to offer against the Volkswagen and in the 1950s Auto Union looked doomed until Daimler-Benz bought it and the Ingolstadt factory was turned over for the production of Mercedes-Benz commercial vehicles. Mercedes scarcely needed the extra capacity, however, and in 1964 the Ingolstadt factory and all of the Auto Union brand names were bought by Volkswagen.

Initially it was the NSU brand within Auto Union that stole attention with its Felix Wankel-designed rotary engine and stylish Ro80 saloon – but the economy and reliability issues blunted its impact. Soon the Auto Union factory was producing Volkswagen-funded cars under the brand name of Audi, thus dividing the German motor industry into its great houses of Daimler-Benz, GM-Opel, Ford of Europe and Volkswagen, with their banner men of BMW making aspirational sports-saloons, Porsche making thoroughbreds and Audi making bread-and-butter cars with no fixed trajectory.

ABOVE One of the projects undertaken by Porsche was the remarkable 1.5-litre, supercharged, four-wheel-drive Cisitalia 360 grand prix car. *(Porsche AG)*

LEFT The original Volkswagen would remain in production until 2003, by which time 21,529,464 were built – from which Porsche earned royalties on every one. *(Volkswagen AG)*

BELOW The Audi 60 and Audi 80 were dowdy cars clad in groovy colours that typified a brand that most people had forgotten about by the mid-1970s. *(Audi AG)*

The man who would be King

The facial similarities between Ferdinand Piëch and his grandfather Ferdinand Porsche are quite uncanny. Unlike his grandfather, however, you would never catch Piëch in a heavy tweed suit and Homburg: his frame has always been rangier and more restless and his dress sense cutting edge.

For all his modern style, the younger man's ambition and temperament have always been a chip off the old block. Years later, when looking back over his own illustrious career, Bob Lutz, the former CEO of General Motors, described Piëch as a 'mad genius' but singled him out as the most influential of his peers, saying that he was: 'Not a person I would particularly want to work for, I think. The autocrat's autocrat. But certainly, personal idiosyncrasies aside, without question I think the greatest living product guy… a detailed, laser-like focus on product excellence and this absolute intolerance of mediocrity in the product.'

A chip off the old block indeed…

When he died, in 1951, Ferdinand Porsche left a vast legacy to his family including a wealth of engineering projects for which the tools and materials were not yet sufficiently advanced, a vast income from royalties on his Volkswagen design and a toxic rift between his daughter Louise's family, the Piëchs, and that of his son Ferry, the Porsches.

There was a silently drawn line between the 'nameholders' and the 'non-nameholders' through which young Ferdinand Piëch gleefully crashed both as a child and as an adult. Nevertheless, the young scion was clearly a bright talent and, having written a thesis about 12-cylinder Formula 1 engines, he duly joined the family firm in the early 1960s.

'We had reliable cars, but to me, as a German, it's a German high school parking lot,' remembered Ralf Friese, from Audi Tradition. 'When the teachers go to lunch, it's Audi 80 in weird colours – some Bahama beige or really crazy green with orange interiors. They're not that stylish at the time. This is Audi: it's a teacher's car.'

All that would change dramatically with the arrival of one man: Ferdinand Piëch.

At that time the first production Porsche, the 356, was 15 years old and Porsche had taken its eye off the ball in sports car racing for an expensive foray into Formula 1 that had borne little fruit. Porsche needed reinvigorating and Piëch was more than willing to play his part as head of research and development by designing a new sports racing car.

He abandoned Porsche's traditional box frame construction in favour of a tubular

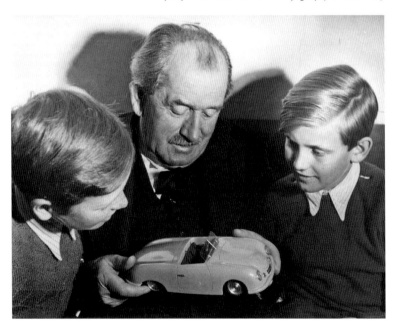

BELOW Ferdinand Porsche and his grandchildren Ferdinand 'Butzi' Porsche (left) and Ferdinand Piëch (right). *(Porsche AG)*

spaceframe, fitting it with a lightweight fibreglass body that was, for the first time, designed using a wind tunnel. The result was called the Porsche 906, and on its debut Piëch's car beat Ferrari for class honours in the 1966 Daytona 24 Hours.

With this success behind him, Piëch decided to steer a course away from Porsche's traditional hunting ground in the small capacity classes and aim for overall victories in the world's great sports car events. The 906 begat the more powerful 907 and 908 models in 1967–68, and soon Porsche was at the sharp end of the grid, winning the 1968 International Cup for GT Cars and the 1969 World Championship for Makes.

Piëch's lust for horsepower went against the grain with those like his uncle Ferry, who had built the firm's reputation on minimalism and from creating performance through engineering rather than brute force. But then so too did it go against the grain when Piëch took a shine to his cousin Gerd Porsche's wife Marlene and wooed her away from the 'named' side of the clan.

Meanwhile, 1969 saw Piëch reveal the ultimate step in his quest for glory: the Porsche 917. With its ear-shattering flat-12 engine and titanium-rich construction, everything about the 917 was bigger, faster and more expensive than ever. It also grew riskier – the early 917s were ferociously unstable at speed, which is not something that drivers admire in a car that could sail past 240 mph. At the 1969 Le Mans 24 Hours, one car crashed fatally on the first lap. How much responsibility for John Woolfe's demise was down to his enthusiasm was a moot point: the drivers were spooked and the Porsche family was worried.

The aerodynamic genius of young designer Norbert Singer produced the revised 917K for 1970, which took Porsche to its first outright victories at the Le Mans 24 Hours in 1970–71 and two successive world championship titles. From 1972, the big 917s were outlawed in

LEFT Ferdinand Porsche's children, Ferry Porsche and Louise Piëch, presided over a growing schism in the family while their company's fortunes prospered. (Porsche AG)

BELOW Ferdinand Piëch first made his mark by creating the Porsche 906 – using state-of-the-art construction methods to revolutionise the firm's competition cars. (Porsche AG)

RIGHT When the large capacity cars were being phased out of endurance racing, Piëch gambled everything on a lavish programme to build the 240+ mph Porsche 917 and dominate the sport. (Porsche AG)

ABOVE After striking out on his own, Ferdinand Piëch developed the OM617 five-cylinder diesel engine for Mercedes-Benz – the power, smoothness and economy of his design creating a sensation. *(Daimler AG)*

Europe but Piëch took the cars to America, added a turbocharger to the flat-12 and created a 1,000 horsepower beast that crushed the opposition in Can-Am racing.

For all of the 917's successes, however, the Porsche family grew deeply concerned by Piëch's increasing expenditure. When the issue was raised, he accused the family of cowardice and declared himself to be a wild boar among domestic pigs.

It is said that this comment was the trigger that led, in 1972, to Ferry Porsche initiating Porsche's transition from a private firm to a publicly held company. In so doing, the Porsche family – or rather the *Piëch* family – would be constitutionally prevented from taking over the overall management of Porsche AG.

Almost as soon as the ink was dry on the

legal documents, Ferdinand Piëch turned his back on Porsche in disgust. Although he retained 10% of the holding company, Piëch, like his grandfather before him, established his own independent design consultancy.

Piëch's first employer in exile was Daimler-Benz, where as a consultant he developed a new five-cylinder inline diesel engine, the OM617. The choice of five cylinders provided smoother, more refined power than the preceding four-cylinder engine, with none of the weight penalties of a six-cylinder. What's more, it was fiendishly reliable, with many Piëch-engined Mercedes seeing a million kilometres (620,000 miles) on their odometer.

The five-cylinder was a triumph but then Piëch wound down his consultancy and accepted a salaried job as head of product development at Audi. With his track record and connections, he could have gone virtually anywhere for a job with more prestige, but by choosing a brand that had sat in the shadows of Mercedes, BMW, Volkswagen, Opel and Porsche for almost half a century, Piëch decided to show the world what he was made of.

The first step came in 1976 when the second-generation Audi 100 was launched. It was more angular and stylish than its predecessor and it boasted a five-cylinder inline gasoline engine, sold with the promise of 'six-cylinder power and four-cylinder economy'. The motoring press fell in love with the new car, its sonorous engine and with the way that the new man at the helm, Ferdinand Piëch, presented

RIGHT The first fruits of Piëch's tenure as head of Audi's product development was the handsome five-cylinder 100 range, which received a rapturous reception. *(Audi AG)*

himself and his army of technicians as cheerful, quirky German geniuses.

It was while enjoying the Audi 100's enormously positive reception that Piëch was confronted by Jörg Bensinger and his plan of developing a high-performance four-wheel-drive car. A year earlier, Porsche had taken the idea of turbocharging that Piëch had introduced with the 917 and run with it: claiming more Le Mans wins and causing a sensation in the production sports car world when the 911 Turbo was unleashed in 1975.

A turbocharged GT car with four-wheel-drive could very well be a more user-friendly and efficient proposition than Porsche's offering. Bensinger's number-crunching showed that in theory a front-engined four-wheel drive car offered better directional stability and traction than a rear-engined rear-wheel-drive car – and with much more benevolent cornering behaviour.

It would cost a lot of money to develop. Furthermore, the unit cost of building a front-engined four-wheel drive would be vast next to the Porsche 911, which was effectively following the same cost-cutting platform as Ferdinand Porsche's Volkswagen.

But cost never deterred Ferdinand Piëch once he had a target. He also knew that motor sport was the best method yet devised for pushing research and development ahead, where change was forced through by the pace and ferocity of competition. What's more, budgets could be subsidised by the manufacturer's marketing spend and by recruiting corporate sponsorship.

It also wouldn't hurt that the world would be watching. A four-wheel-drive GT car might just be the sword that Piëch could wield to reclaim his throne. If it was, he would want the Porsches to see him coming.

The Quattro brotherhood

With Ferdinand Piëch's unofficial blessing secured, Jörg Bensinger then had to turn his theories into reality. To do so would need an engineer of some skill, but Roland Gumpert was still tied up with the Iltis programme, which meant that Bensinger would have to call upon someone else's services. Whoever joined Bensinger's team in February 1977 would have

ABOVE Piëch had spearheaded turbocharging at Porsche, taking the 917 to unprecedented heights. In 1975 the Porsche 930 road car brought turbo technology to the high street. *(Porsche AG)*

to build and test a new concept in complete secrecy, and the chosen man to lead the build was Walter Treser.

The 37-year-old was a racer and engineer who had competed as a BMW driver in the European Touring Car Championship before becoming a development engineer at Pirelli. Treser had only recently arrived at Audi but he had all the credentials needed for the job of exploring what potential there was for four-wheel drive with regard to tyre wear and performance. 'I simply liked the idea of developing a vision for a car in a form that didn't

BELOW Walter Treser was handed the responsibility for engineering a four-wheel-drive Audi, and in complete secrecy he led a tiny hand-picked team. *(McKlein)*

exist at that time,' Treser remembered. 'And to show the world that we could do it better.'

The first test hack was made during March 1977, using a two-door Audi 80 bodyshell that was painted in a nondescript shade of red with a black vinyl roof – outwardly every inch the 'teacher's car'. But the lessons that this example, code-named A1, would teach were rather more engaging than Year 9 Geography.

Because the project was even secret within Audi it was impossible for Treser's team of Frankensteins to outsource parts for their monster or have new parts drawn up and made. This meant that parts needed to be improvised from existing stocks and the man who knew most about the Audi parts bin and how to bastardise its contents was a veteran engineer called Hans Nedvidek. He had cut his teeth on the Mercedes-Benz Formula 1 team of the 1950s and if parts needed modifying or fabricating to suit the A1 then Nedvidek got it done.

Quite who fathered the hollow transmission shaft that allowed the front and rear wheels to be driven without a transfer box has not been answered definitively. The four-wheel drive sat under Bensinger, while transmission engineer Franz Tengler is cited by Audi as the man who conjured the fix, while Quattro authority Jeremy Walton understood from his visits to the factory early in the car's life that it was the redoubtable Hans Nedvidek who had fabricated almost all of the modifications.

Ultimately, credit for the entire creation of

Audi's four-wheel-drive system rests between 12 engineers who worked in secret for five months. Their handiwork would come to redefine the Audi brand, the parameters of road car handling and eventually the sport of rallying.

Once Piëch had sampled and approved of the illegitimate car's qualities there was only one thing to do: it was time for the A1 to be revealed. So it was that the little red Audi 80 was presented internally to the senior staff at Audi as less of a *fait accompli* and more as a source of wonderment in the autumn of 1977, with a slightly tongue-in-cheek sense of: 'Oh look! How did this get here! Good heavens!'

Fortunately for the career prospects of all concerned, the very obvious potential within Bensinger's A1 development hack delighted Audi's management. An official request was made for the four-wheel-drive prototype to be designated EA 262 (short for Entwickung Auftrag or development project), and with the green light shining overhead it was time to turn the humble A1 into a performance motoring legend.

Fire on the ice

The original engine was removed from A1 and in its place the new turbocharged 2.2-litre, five-cylinder powerplant from the flagship Audi 200 was squeezed in. Developing the turbocharged high-performance car to Ferdinand Piëch's exacting standards would take until January 1978, when the senior managers of Audi were invited to cross Obersalzberg into Austria and the snowy Gurktal Alps, where the full potential of EA 262 would be theirs to sample.

The Turracher Höhe is one of the steepest passes on the mountainside, with the road reaching 23 degrees of elevation in places. Before the top brass arrived, the man whose reputation rested upon the success of their outing also took a drive.

'Piëch was behind the wheel of one of our first prototypes and when the car came to a stop at the Turracher Höhe mountain pass, local people were there fitting snow chains,' Walter Treser recalled. 'And then, while assembling the snow chains, the locals kept glancing at the [Audi] with its summer tyres with expressions of pity on their faces. They fitted snow chains and then Piëch just sped off on summer tyres through the swirling snow.'

When the time came, EA 262 repeated its performance in the hands of Volkswagen sales director Dr Werner Schmidt and marketing director Edgar von Schenck. Wide-eyed at the experience, the combined might of Audi and Volkswagen management then sat round a table in the Alps and thrashed out the next course of action. Ferdinand Piëch, aided by his lieutenants, took control of the situation.

Piëch suggested that the turbocharged four-wheel-drive car should be built using the forthcoming Audi Coupé as its basis. This, he reasoned, would make the more stylish halo vehicle and it would serve as a better basis for a competition car, while still utilising the new B2 platform that would go under the Audi Coupé, Audi 80, Audi 90 and Volkswagen Passat. Only 400 examples of this special version would be needed to get the required FIA homologation to enter their magnificent four-wheel-drive supercar in the World Rally Championship, where it would compete on ice and snow, on gravel tracks and on paved roads against relatively simple cars like the Ford Escort and Saab 99.

Despite the tantalising success of their drive up Turracher Höhe, Piëch met some resistance from the senior staff towards his plan. For one thing, the coupé was already a prestige model in the Audi range that was not yet launched – usurping it with an expensive high-

performance version did not make commercial sense. Moreover, the management was not convinced that they could sell 400 examples of an expensive supercar. Piëch prevailed only in getting their agreement to continue testing prototypes with the Audi 80 body alongside a handful of coupé examples.

While Treser and his fast-expanding team got to work on the prototypes, many meetings were held on how to sell the idea of a high-performance four-wheel-drive car to the public.

ABOVE Audi launched its own turbocharged car – the Audi 200 – from which the basis of the Quattro's powerplant would be drawn. *(Audi AG)*

BELOW Audi had intended to launch the coupé as a premium model in its own right, but instead it became the donor car to the Quattro and was released after its more muscular four-wheel-drive sibling. *(Audi AG)*

RIGHT The prototype
Audi Quattros were
tested relentlessly
in the Austrian Alps,
where type approval
was thrashed out, as
well as in the Sahara
and a local gravel pit
in Bavaria. *(Audi AG)*

The performance version of the coupé had to
look different to the standard model. It also had
to comply with the body dimensions permitted
by the Fédération Internationale de Sport Auto
(FISA), the world's sanctioning body for motor
sport, in order to compete in the FIA World Rally
Championship.

The job of styling Ferdinand Piëch's supercar
was handed to a young Englishman called
Martin Smith. 'The design of the coupé that the
Quattro was based on was basically finalised
when I arrived, so my brief was to make the
Quattro look technical, to stress that it was the
first 4x4 performance car,' he later said.

'I worked with a design model, and changed
the fenders, the front end and the rear spoiler.
I also came up with the flared arches… We
submitted the final model to Toni Schmücker
[then Volkswagen board chairman] for approval
and I remember it was in metallic white and the
Audi rings on the side were in orange.'

Another great question to be resolved was
what the finished car was going to be called.
For a project that was so precious to them,
the engineers did not want Volkswagen's
marketing men to have the final call and when
word reached them that the name Volkswagen
was keenest on was Carat, the measure
of gemstones and precious metals, the
development team was appalled – Carat was a
low-cost women's perfume!

'I tried the whole time to find a name
that was not just a name but more a type of

classification,' Treser recalled. 'And then we
came up with Quattro – with two t's and an r
that rolled off the tongue much better.'

At the first opportunity, Treser and Bensinger
went to the Volkswagen marketing men armed
with Ferdinand Piëch's blessing and a scale
model of Martin Smith's handiwork. 'The name
Carat was presented in this meeting, I said:
"Surely you don't want to name this beautiful
car after an ordinary women's cologne?" I
showed them the model, which didn't make
me any friends, but in the end it helped make
sure that Quattro won out,' Treser said with
a chuckle.

In April 1978 a coupé-bodied Audi was
transported in secrecy to the Hockenheimring
circuit, newly established as the home of
the German Grand Prix. Also present was a
Porsche 928, which packed a punch of 240
bhp to the 160 bhp then being put out by the
prototype Audi. Despite the endless straights
that have sadly been shorn from Hockenheim's
majestic layout, the two cars lapped at almost
an identical time thanks to the huge difference
in cornering speed.

One month later, in May 1978, the
boardroom fell. All of Piëch's demands would
be met – there would be an initial production
of 400 coupés called the Audi Quattro and
there would be an entry in the World Rally
Championship from which to showcase the
technological marvel that his team had created.
An in-house competition department was

Quattro or quattro?

Writing a book about a subject like the Audi Quattro is a daunting prospect, primarily because German cars, above all others, inspire such devotion. Whether it is Audi, BMW or Porsche, every specific sub-type, trim stripe and wiring loom is common knowledge to the cognoscenti – upon which the credibility of the end product will hinge.

Some things are basic enough: the original 2,144 cc 10-valve engine is the WR, the later 2,226 cc Group B homologation engines being the MB (10-valve) and RR (20-valve). But if ever you wish to enter a motoring bearpit, try the nomenclature of the Audi Quattro. At times it is like negotiating, like Monty Python's *Life of Brian*, between the People's Front of Judea and the Judean People's Front.

Read any coverage of rallies from 1981–86 and the Audi *Quattro* is mentioned, its 'Q' proudly capitalised whether in long or short wheelbase form. Of course the shorter cars of 1984 onwards were also called the Audi Sport Quattro. But what of the final, iconic monster? Audi Quattro S1? Audi Quattro S1 E2? Audi quattro E2?

In the British media particularly, the old standard has been that the original coupé of 1980–91 should be called the Quattro, as it is a noun, but that thereafter all later four-wheel-drive cars such as the Audi 200 quattro and Audi A4 quattro should be lower case as an adjective describing the transmission system. But in fact this is not so.

Thanks to the good offices of Franz Lang and the IG-Audi Sport team, comprised of original team members, much original documentation for the rally cars has been produced, and it is to these that this work will show deference. In the workshop nobody ever said 'have you got a spare bonnet for an S1 E2?' and if you use such terminology today you get a raised eyebrow and a sigh. The short wheelbase car was the Sport quattro and the winged car the S1. So it is that for the remainder of the book, the following terms will be used:

- Group 4 (1981–82): **Audi Quattro**
- Group B (1983–86, long wheelbase): **Audi Quattro** (suffix **A1** or **A2**)
- Group B (1984–86, short wheelbase): **Audi Sport quattro**
- Group B (1985–86, redesigned short wheelbase): **Audi Sport quattro S1**
- The term 'Ur-Quattro' (Ur being the primitive ancestor to modern cattle in Europe), has become popular among enthusiasts in recent years, after the phrase was once used by Jörg Bensinger and then proliferated via the Internet. If you're a keyboard-wielding car guy then you know what an Ur-Quattro is but the phrase is much more recent than the cars that it describes… and describing a car like the Quattro in bovine terms seems somewhat disrespectful, unless you happen to be Jörg Bensinger.

Here endeth the lesson!

LEFT It's a Quattro. Sometimes spelt quattro. *(Author)*

Audi. But if the public was suddenly wild about this elegant sports-coupé, it is easy to imagine the shockwaves that it sent through FISA and the manufacturers competing in the FIA World Rally Championship because this was decidedly not the sort of thing that they had been expecting at all...

1973–1980: Apprenticeship

The start of Audi's modern motor sport programme came in 1973, when a prize fund was inaugurated for private entrants who competed in races and rallies in Audi cars. To help manage this programme and create a link between the teams and those back at the factory servicing their needs, Audi hired former Solex carburettor engineer and man-about-paddock Jürgen Stockmar as a combined competitors' liaison-cum-salesman. By 1978, Audi was ready to enter the World Rally Championship as a toe-in-the-water exercise with its immaculate front-wheel-drive 80s being run with support from the workshops of Schmidt Motorsport.

duly founded, making its home in a former supermarket warehouse just outside Ingolstadt.

The Audi Quattro road cars would not be revealed to the world until the 1980 Geneva Motor Show, where in glistening pearlescent white paintwork the concept wrapped brilliantly within Martin Smith's elegant coachwork left onlookers flabbergasted. Despite a price of DM49,900 – two-and-a-half times that of the Audi Coupé – in the end, all 400 of the original cars were sold swiftly. In fact, the Quattro would remain in production until 1991 by which time more than 11,000 of them had been built.

The road car's story was one of pure success based upon that moment in Geneva when the world finally sat up and took notice of

Stockmar presided over the team, supported by former Volkswagen Motorsport marketing man Reinhard Rode. Bavarian-Swedish nobleman Freddy Kottulinsky was lead driver, joined by talented youngster Harald Demuth in the second car. Although retirements were regular, the Audis

began to log a number of top-five finishes when they held together long enough.

There was still one rather large hurdle for Audi to cross before the Quattro could begin its competitive career. One of which, it must be assumed, the Audi board was not aware when it signed off Piëch's proposed Quattro road car and World Rally Championship assault in May 1978: four-wheel-drive cars were not permitted in the series.

In the late summer of 1979, Volkswagen announced that it would enter the 1980 Paris–Dakar marathon with its Iltis four-wheel drive. The man tasked with making the cars ready for Dakar was none other than Roland Gumpert, who later remembered: 'We tried to get orders from different armies, so we decided to participate in the 1980 Paris-Dakar to convince them how good the Iltis was!'

Convincing generals that the Iltis was a sound purchase was certainly one objective behind planning the Dakar mission, but almost as certainly, another aim was to draw attention away from the as-yet unseen Quattro.

In September 1979, Stockmar represented Audi in the meeting of manufacturers held at the FIA headquarters on the Place de la Concorde in Paris. He played little part in the most volatile conversations that ebbed and flowed throughout the day as the foundations were laid for the future specification of rallying: Group A production cars and the more technically liberal category of Group B.

When the horse trading over production numbers and specifications was over, Stockmar spoke up to ask if the other manufacturers would support lifting the ban on four-wheel-drive cars in rallying. With all the talk about the Iltis and Dakar that was emanating from Germany at the time, it was assumed by the rest of the gathering that Volkswagen hoped to enter its Jeep in similar rough-and-tumble events like the Safari Rally.

With no hint of the coming storm, Stockmar's motion was given unanimous support from the manufacturers. Not until the road-going Quattro was unveiled at the Geneva Motor Show, some six months later, did a sense of unease afflict the Audi's rivals.

Stockmar was meanwhile preoccupied with recruiting a driver of sufficient calibre to make

ABOVE By launching one of the first major manufacturer assaults on the Paris–Dakar Rally with the Iltis, Volkswagen and Audi kept other manufacturers in the dark about the Quattro rally programme. *(Audi AG)*

best use of the Quattro. Luck was with Audi in that Ford announced its withdrawal from the world championship as a full manufacturer at the end of 1979, putting the services of men like Björn Waldegård (who would win the inaugural drivers' title that year), Finnish veteran Hannu Mikkola and his spectacular young compatriot Ari Vatanen on the market.

From this list of candidates, Audi zeroed in on Hannu Mikkola as their first choice. 'I said I wasn't so sure, but they had a list of the drivers

BELOW After the Iltis dominated the Dakar, Audi unveiled the Quattro road cars at the Geneva motor show to worldwide acclaim. *(Audi AG)*

RIGHT Germany's first
world rally champion,
Walter Röhrl, chose to
join the fledgling rally
team at Mercedes-
Benz over Audi. It
sparked a war that
would cost Audi two
world championship
titles. (McKlein)

who they thought could drive the car and they
said I was the only one,' Mikkola later said.
'They'd been following my career at Ford and
discovered that I drove less sideways, and said
it had to be me.'

Mikkola flew to Ingolstadt where he was met
by Stockmar, shown around the factory and
given a road-going Quattro prototype to drive.
Mikkola was unsure about making such a leap
into the unknown, so he called Arne Hertz for
his opinion and then slept on the idea. The
following morning, an agreement was made:

'I said: "Okay, if we can do it so that I
can drive 1980 with which car I want (not an
Audi), but I do 60 days testing and you have
somebody who is doing the long-distance
testing",' Mikkola recalled. He eventually signed
a contract on the understanding that if by
October 1980 the car was not competitive, he
could walk away without penalty.

Almost as soon as Mikkola's signature had
been won, however, Stockmar was fired after
a disagreement with Ferdinand Piëch. He was
immediately replaced by Walter Treser, while
Gumpert and the Audi-prepared Iltis team set
off on the Paris–Dakar event.

Four cars were entered for the Dakar,
although Freddy Kottulinsky had no real wish
to compete and so put in an extraordinarily
high price for his services in the hope of being
turned down. Eventually Volkswagen agreed to
his terms and then Kottulinsky went on to win
the event, with his teammates Patrick Zaniroli
finishing second and Jean Ragnotti fourth. Even
Gumpert managed to finish ninth overall in the
'chase car' Iltis that was used to keep a stock
of spare parts and skilled labour close at hand!

Back in Ingolstadt, Walter Treser's school
of leadership was soon making waves. For
one thing, he informed Schmidt Motorsport
that its services would no longer be required:
the Quattro could be managed perfectly well
by men drawn from the production line. For
another, Treser spurned experienced suppliers
for many of the rally team's needs: French
tyre brand Kleber, Boge shock absorbers and
Pierburg fuel injection, for example.

Treser's unshakeable faith in the Quattro also
played a part in the negotiations with Walter
Röhrl. The German superstar visited Ingolstadt
twice – and each time he left with no contract
signed. Immediately after his second visit, Röhrl
went to Stuttgart and agreed terms for a five-
year contract with Mercedes-Benz. Treser did
not take the snub well, publicly declaring Röhrl
a 'Bavarian twit' and lighting an incandescent
rage in the driver that would haunt Audi for
years to come.

Without Röhrl another bankable star was
needed to drive the team's second car and

Audi's marketing team felt that a French driver would help them in a key market for sales. In the end they recruited another driver who was competing with Fiat in 1980 – and this one happened to be a woman. 'English was hard for me then, so I went to Ingolstadt with a translator,' Michèle Mouton recalled. 'I was driving for Fiat, but they let me go to a test in Finland. After the test I signed a contract. The Fiat 131 was like a truck in comparison.'

By the autumn of 1980, Audi was ready to show the world the results of its long and secretive labours. Hannu Mikkola and his co-driver Arne Hertz would attend the Algarve Rally in Portugal, part of the FIA European Rally Championship calendar, where the Quattro would act as course car.

'The first stage was uphill, I think 24km [15 miles] or something, and we knew our times from the last year,' Mikkola later said. 'Arne was with me and we went up the stage and we were one minute faster than in the Escort. We knew then that it was a good car, and it was quite easy to drive, so I could see that maybe this was the way to go.'

In the end, the course car covered the 30 timed stages half an hour faster than the Porsche 911 that won the event, setting 24 fastest stage times along the way. A veritable scrum of international media was in attendance at a fairly low-key event. What they wrote was largely awestruck about the speed that the Quattros possessed – if not the spectacle. Mikkola's Quattro had simply driven around each corner under complete control and then shot off with a big burst of acceleration. The technical brilliance of the car was clear, but to many onlookers the big question mark that Mikkola's performance posed was whether the Quattro could be loved. They would soon have an answer.

BELOW The Quattro gave notice of Audi's intent late in the 1980 season with a handful of appearances as a course car on the FIA European Rally Championship – staggering onlookers with its speed. Here Hannu Mikkola thunders through the Algarve. *(McKlein)*

Chapter Two

The competition story

The competition programme for the Audi Quattro was defined by the rallies of Monte Carlo, the Acropolis, the 1,000 Lakes and the RAC, upon which millions of spectators converged to glimpse the biggest stars and the wildest cars ever seen in the sport's history. From 1981 to 1986 the tempo of rallying rose to dizzying levels, as did the budgets and the hysteria – and Audi was right in the thick of it all throughout.

OPPOSITE A sporting icon: the sight of an Audi Quattro right on the limit, within touching distance of thousands of fans on every special stage, became a defining image of the 1980s. (McKlein)

ABOVE **First blood was drawn by Franz Wittmann and Kurt Nestinger when they won the Jänner Rallye in Austria, a European series event, by a colossal margin.** *(McKlein)*

The 1981 World Rally Championship

The final preparatory run for the Audi Quattro would also be its first competitive appearance, when Franz Wittmann and co-driver Dr Kurt Nestinger lined up for the start of Austria's Jänner Rallye in January 1981. In the snowy conditions the car performed faultlessly, winning every one of the 31 stages to finish 20 minutes ahead of John Haughland's little Škoda 120. Now it was time for Audi to enter the big league.

Each World Rally Championship season traditionally begins in Monte Carlo. Audi set off from a ceremonial start in Bad Homburg with two Quattros for Mikkola/Hertz and Mouton/Pons, together with their flotilla of service vehicles. They joined a cavalcade that included works Renault 5 Turbos, Opel Asconas, Talbot Sunbeams and a Datsun Violet plus a host of rapid privateer Ford Escorts, Fiat 131s, Porsche 911s and a lone Lancia Stratos for Bernard Darniche.

The cream of rallying was out on the sport's blue riband event but soon Mikkola had thrown down the gauntlet. 'We did the first stage quite near Grenoble: short one, 14km [9 miles], but all the way uphill nearly and I remember Darniche started in front of me, one minute in front of me, and when I had done 7km I passed him like anything,' the Finn later recalled.

'When we came to the start of the next stage Ari [Vatanen] pulled next to me… with David Richards who used to be his co-driver – they had a bet what was my time. Nobody really knew how well the car will go and Dave Richards said that I did the same than the best time and Ari said "you were ten seconds faster than best time" and I remember very well I said "yes you are quite right… but I was 1 minute 10 seconds faster than next one". So that was a real shock for everybody.'

It was less of a dream start for Michèle Mouton, who was forced to retire with contaminated fuel bunging up her motor. Mikkola, meanwhile, rocketed through the stages, an average 2.5 seconds faster per kilometre than anyone else in the field. Then his luck changed, first of all crashing when he attempted to left-foot brake in a corner and then, following a hasty repair, he crashed again when a poorly fitted steering arm fell apart. The third and final crash occurred when his brake pedal fell to bits, allowing Frenchman Jean Ragnotti through to win for Renault in front of a hysterically partisan crowd.

The next stop would be Sweden, where Audi sent just one car for Mikkola as no manufacturers' points were on offer. This time the weekend ran according to plan as the Finn won 15 out of 25 stages to beat fellow countryman Ari Vatanen's privately entered Ford Escort by two minutes to become the first non-Swedish winner in the event's history.

BELOW **In the Alpes Maritimes on the Monte Carlo Rally, Hannu Mikkola set astonishing times on the Quattro's World Rally Championship debut before technical problems hobbled his charge.** *(McKlein)*

Moving from snow to gravel saw Mikkola retire from the next round in Portugal with a broken engine while Mouton logged her first points by finishing fourth. Audi didn't go to the Safari Rally, then on the next outing in Corsica both cars went out with blown engines after struggling for pace on the tortuous asphalt roads.

To the rally establishment it looked as though Audi had bitten off more than it could chew. The cars were getting progressively lighter but the Quattro was still a big beast next to the Escorts, Talbots and similar. Turbocharging gave its sonorous five-cylinder plenty of power but it added complexity and frailty to the car.

Audi Sport's next outing was in Greece for the Acropolis Rally, where Mouton and Mikkola were joined by Franz Wittmann in a third car. Things began to go wrong when two of the team's recce cars suffered from overheating problems. To aid cooling on the rally cars, therefore, the inner pair of standard headlights was removed and replaced by a flap that opened under air pressure to cool the engine bay. This was not a homologated part but the cars passed through scrutineering without issue.

Michèle Mouton led at the start but then as she left service one of the mechanics noticed that her left rear suspension was coming apart. It was too late to fix it and she duly ended the next leg on three wheels and way down the order.

At the next service, Walter Treser got under Mikkola's car to check for similar issues, but while he was down there one of the mechanics decided to refuel the car. Fuel slopped over the battery, exhaust and over the prone figure of Treser… and because Audi kept its engines running at service halts the whole lot instantly went up in flames.

Arne Hertz jumped in to the flaming Quattro and moved it away from Treser so that both the car and their team boss could be doused. There was minimal damage to the Audi but Treser suffered significant burns to his hands and face – although he remained at his post. Mikkola went on to take the lead but then the rally officials stepped in and declared Audi's modified headlight openings to be illegal, with the additional charge of having carried a spare battery in the driver's foot well. Denied an appeal and fined 25,000 drachmas for its trouble, Audi Sport was sent home in disgrace.

Walter Treser was quietly removed from Audi Sport while he recuperated, with the loyal lieutenant Reinhard Rode being promoted and Roland Gumpert taking the technical reins. Gumpert's first job was to work with the team's homologation engineer Jürgen Bertl to get a more effective radiator grille approved, featuring a pronounced overbite and just one standard headlamp on each side.

The next round was the 1,000 Lakes in Finland, around the fast, sweeping gravel and spectacular yumps. Mikkola rocketed into the lead early on while Mouton clouted a rock and tumbled down the order, but worse was in store for Franz Wittmann. The popular Austrian was unsighted by heavy rain and vast numbers of spectators who obscured signs showing the end-of-stage slowing down area. Too late he

ABOVE The Quattro's first victory came in its second event, and made Mikkola the first non-Swede to win the Swedish Rally. *(McKlein)*

BELOW Disaster struck Walter Treser and his team repeatedly on the Acropolis – including being declared illegal for the flaps fitted in place of the inner headlights. Treser was quietly moved aside thereafter. *(McKlein)*

BELOW **History is written: Michèle Mouton became the first woman to win a world championship event outright in Sanremo, taking command of the event entirely.** *(McKlein)*

BOTTOM **The 1981 season ended on a high note with Mikkola marching off to victory on the RAC Rally, despite rolling his car along the way.** *(McKlein)*

saw a group of officials in his way and was powerless to avoid hitting the men, of whom Raul Falin, president of the Finnish Automobile Association, later died.

A police inquiry was launched as the officials contradicted Wittmann's version of events entirely, but he was subsequently exonerated from blame by the police. Mikkola's engine meanwhile dropped a cylinder and he could do little to hold back Ari Vatanen's flying Escort, eventually finishing third. Finland had been a baptism of fire for Rode and Gumpert's leadership, who would spend the next few weeks furiously getting improved engine components designed and tested before heading to Italy's Sanremo Rally.

In Italy, Walter Röhrl was in commanding form at the wheel of a Porsche 911 on asphalt but then the rally switched over to gravel and the heavily revised Quattros began to shine. Audi's third car was being run for local youngster Michele Cinotto, who took maximum advantage of a lowly road position to allow the front runners to sweep away the loosest gravel and give him an ideal surface.

Cinotto took the lead but then it was his job to do the sweeping and, in frustration, he began to get a bit wild in front of such a passionate home crowd. He crashed. Twice. Cinotto's dramas allowed Michèle Mouton to the fore, who was revelling in the performance of her revised Quattro and pulling away from Vatanen, Röhrl, Mikkola and all the rest. As she crossed the line on the final stage she etched her name in the history books for all time as the first woman ever to win a world championship event in any branch of motor sport… and the crowd went wild.

Audi missed the Ivory Coast Rally and so only the final round of the season remained: Britain's RAC Rally, where Hannu Mikkola was traditionally on sublime form. There was no hope of winning the championships – the drivers' title race was between Vatanen in David Sutton's Ford Escort and Guy Fréquelin in the works Talbot Sunbeam Lotus. It would take a strong finish from Fréquelin and misfortune for Vatanen to deny the Finn, but with reliability Talbot could beat Datsun to the manufacturers' crown.

None of this mattered to Mikkola, who simply drove away from everyone. Such was his urgency to end the season on a high that the Finn rolled his car in Grizedale forest and temporarily allowed home-grown hero Tony Pond through to lead. The damage was only cosmetic, however, and Mikkola soon regained his stride in the taped-together Quattro to win by 11 minutes from new drivers' champion Vatanen, while Saab refugee Stig Blomqvist took third for Talbot and sealed its manufacturers' championship win.

The 1982 FIA World Rally Championship

The 1981 season had been a bruising one for Audi Sport, but there was no time to be mawkish. When the 1981 RAC Rally ended, there were just seven weeks until the start of the 1982 Monte Carlo Rally, of which four weeks were to be taken up with the pre-event

recce. That gave Roland Gumpert little time to get his house in order.

It was clear that Gumpert was relishing the job of leading the team and that the staff and drivers all felt happier under his command. In 1982, Audi's national markets would begin to launch their own domestic Quattro rally programmes with support from the Ingolstadt team and so Reinhard Rode was moved across to manage their needs. This gave Gumpert dominion over the whole world championship programme.

The other big change was that FISA was now opening entries for Group B cars. Rather grudgingly, the manufacturers had been granted a year's stay of execution on their Group 4 cars if they were prepared to commit to Group B and to building the 200 road-going examples needed for homologation purposes. Thus the 1982 Monte Carlo Rally would be marked down as the starting point of a new era – even if Group B was only populated by a couple of Porsche 911s and some small-capacity Citroën Visas.

Audi Sport entered two Quattros for Mikkola/ Hertz and Mouton/Pons, with Michele Cinotto and co-driver Emilio Radaelli entered with support from David Sutton Cars, which had been brought in to run the British and Italian domestic championship entries, while Schmidt Motorsport was back to run entries in German and Austrian competition. Unlike Walter Treser, Gumpert was quite happy to work with more experienced rally men and feed ideas and experience back and forth.

If all was a bed of roses within the organisation, however, it soon became clear that this Monte Carlo Rally was not going to go Audi's way. With precious little snow on the ground, a significant advantage was handed back to the lighter and nimbler two-wheel-drive cars – most notably the Opel Ascona of Walter Röhrl.

Flinging his Opel around the bone-dry asphalt, Röhrl proved insuperable. Hannu Mikkola was happy to finish second under the circumstances but first Michele Cinotto crashed, then Mouton hit a house with such force that Fabrizia Pons was knocked out cold and had to be helicoptered off the stage for a check-up.

The next round was Sweden, which saw Stig Blomqvist make his first start for Audi in the world championship. From the moment that Blomqvist first drove the Quattro he was at home: its understeering nature and the throttle

lag inherent with turbocharged engines were familiar from his Saab days.

On the first day in Sweden, fuel injection issues dropped Blomqvist down to 113th overall. Even a five-time winner of the event would have swallowed hard at recovering that much ground, but by the second leg he was up to third place behind Mikkola and the Ford Escort of Ari Vatanen, with Mouton just behind him.

When Vatanen's car gave out underneath him, Blomqvist was expected to ride shotgun to Mikkola and help Audi bank maximum points from a 1-2-3 finish. But then Mikkola relaxed too much and speared his Quattro into a snow bank in the dying stages of the rally. Blomqvist was first on the scene and just squeezed through the gap but Mouton was not so lucky: ploughing into the rear end of Mikkola's car and burying it completely in the bank.

BELOW Revenge is a dish best served cold. After a year on the sidelines, Walter Röhrl took on the Quattros with an icy fury in 1982 – starting his 1982 Opel campaign with victory in Monte Carlo. *(McKlein)*

BOTTOM Michèle Mouton crashed heavily on the Monte, requiring co-driver Fabrizia Pons to be helicoptered to hospital. *(McKlein)*

ABOVE Employed by Audi's Swedish importer, front-wheel drive specialist Stig Blomqvist was the first driver to grab the Quattro by the scruff of the neck – taking victory on his home round of the world championship. *(McKlein)*

ABOVE RIGHT When the Portugal Rally got on the gravel, Mikkola went off but Mouton soared, pulling away from the likes of Röhrl and Vatanen to claim an emphatic win. *(McKlein)*

RIGHT Quattros were always hard work on the Tour de Corse – here a beleaguered Mouton grabs refreshment. *(McKlein)*

Thus for the sixth time in his career, Stig Blomqvist won the Swedish Rally. Michèle Mouton's redesigned car struggled home fifth, while Hannu Mikkola and Arne Hertz had to dig their cars out and could only finish 16th. Audi's team leader now trailed their guest driver in the world championship standings… but next would be Portugal and a chance to get even on gravel.

On the early asphalt stages Mikkola lay second: in front of Walter Röhrl's Opel, but behind the second Ascona entered for young Finnish charger Henri Toivonen. No matter: by far the most stage miles would be run on gravel and Mikkola could confidently look forward to catching his young compatriot.

An Audi would indeed win in Portugal but it was Michèle Mouton who took the honours rather than Mikkola. The Finn had rolled his Quattro down a hillside into retirement, leaving Mouton to pull away relentlessly from the rest of the field while the third Quattro of Franz Wittmann clawed its way up the order to finish third.

For the second year running, Audi decided to skip the Safari Rally, which was won by the African specialists of Datsun (now rebranded Nissan), but a dogged performance had seen Walter Röhrl finish second. There was still plenty of the season remaining and Audi was right behind Opel in the manufacturers' standings, but Röhrl was now more than 30 points clear of Mikkola and only Mouton stood a realistic chance of catching him.

The hot, tortuous asphalt of Corsica was never an ally of the Quattros. Jean Ragnotti won for Renault and France duly celebrated, while Mikkola went out with gearbox failure and Wittmann crashed, leaving Mouton as the last Quattro standing, down in seventh place. Two places behind her was Markku Alén in the first appearance of a Lancia built to the new Group B rally formula: the 037 Rallye. It was feather-light and fragile but it was a thing of beauty to behold.

A big, muscular German car with four-wheel drive was precisely the vehicle that was needed on the Acropolis Rally, however, which would be the next round of the championship. Hannu Mikkola arrived still with just the 15 points he had scored in Monte Carlo; less than half the tally of Mouton and just over a quarter that of Röhrl. He would leave Greece without adding to his score after hitting a rock on the second timed stage that caused his Quattro to be mortally wounded.

Two more Quattros would go lame on the event: Franz Wittmann breaking his steering and Michele Cinotto suffering electrical gremlins. The surviving Quattro belonged to

Michèle Mouton, with Fabrizia Pons alongside her, and she would eventually take victory in a tense battle with Röhrl.

The whole world was now pulling for Mouton to win the championship, but at Audi Sport the manufacturers' title would always have to come first. This didn't matter to the press, who relished a battle between Audi's female star and the hard-nosed Röhrl – and it first got feisty when Mouton won again in the Greek sunshine.

Walter Röhrl later remembered: 'Before the Acropolis – which she won – I took Werner Grissmann, the famous downhill skier, up a gravel road with hairpins in the Opel and he asked, "Could anything be quicker?" I said: "A monkey in a Quattro," meaning that the Quattro had so much power and traction that anyone could drive it quicker than the Opel up that hill. But, as often happens, it got around that I had compared Michèle to a monkey…'

It was a long haul to New Zealand for the next competitive outing and Gumpert decided to hand over the reins to David Sutton, who would run the works cars in order to minimise disruption to the works team and its development programme. Gumpert didn't miss much: Mikkola's steering failed and Mouton's car sprung a terminal oil leak. The new Toyota Celicas of Björn Waldegård and Per Eklund finished 1-2 while behind them was Röhrl, assiduously gathering 12 very valuable points.

The next round was supposed to have been in Argentina but fallout from the Falklands War precluded such fripperies and so Brazil stepped into the breach as a host. This was also to be the first event at which the Audi Quattros would be classified as Group B machines.

Although no modifications had been made,

Gumpert and his team had satisfied FISA that it would be ready and willing to enter fully Group B compliant Quattros from the start of 1983. Plans had been laid for both a modified standard car and a short wheelbase version to try and make the Quattro more competitive in Corsica if needed, which satisfied FISA and thus the current Group 4 cars were given Group B status for the rest of the season.

With its paperwork thus in order, Brazil provided another event to forget for Hannu Mikkola, who crashed. It was a quirky little event, run somewhat haphazardly but featuring some of the most jaw-dropping scenery ever seen in the world championship – and it was an event that Mouton relished. Hers would be another knock-down-drag-out contest with Walter Röhrl, but the battle ended in her third win of the season.

From this point onwards, Röhrl was going

ABOVE The Brazil
Rally was a rather
amateurish event
and hard work for
the crews, but the
momentum was with
Audi. *(McKlein)*

BELOW On the 1,000
Lakes, the team
opted to distribute the
optimal tyres between
local hero Mikkola
and hard-charging
Blomqvist – to much
French chagrin.
(McKlein)

to have to start dropping his worst scores of the season, giving Mouton every incentive to push hard. It should also have galvanised the Audi Sport team around her to beat their outspoken nemesis, but with Opel still leading the manufacturers' points table, Gumpert had to ensure maximum points in all the remaining rallies, the first of which was in Finland for the 1,000 Lakes.

Audi put Stig Blomqvist out in the third works car to help its cause. Walter Röhrl was not in attendance as he did not care for the Finnish event but if Mouton was to capitalise on his absence she would need to keep on terms not only with Mikkola and Blomqvist but also local heroes Henri Toivonen in the lead Opel entry and Markku Alén in Lancia's Group B supercar.

Adding to her concerns, Mouton would also have to be content with running on Kleber's lesser tyres while Blomqvist brought a stash

of the Michelin tyres that he had been using in the Swedish championship and Mikkola, eager to lose no advantage at home, was also given Michelins. Mikkola and Mouton were neck-and-neck in the early stages and although the Frenchwoman was having to work much harder on lesser rubber, it would be a brave man who suggested to Hannu Mikkola that he back off on the 1,000 Lakes.

Both of Audi's regular drivers were embroiled in a mighty scrap with Toivonen, Alén and Ari Vatanen. Blomqvist had meanwhile shot off into a sizeable lead. Alén's Lancia broke down early on but then Mouton, trying everything to stay with her teammates, broke the front differential on a jump and only realised that she had a two-wheel-drive Quattro at the next bend as she went off.

The car was not badly damaged despite rolling, and Finland is full of eager fans who bring tow rope and muscle in ample supply. But by that stage Mouton had seen enough of the rally and the perceived lack of parity with her teammates, so she left the car in its ditch. That was a shame because third place was the very least that she could have achieved.

As it was, Blomqvist had a similar moment on the same stage and fell back into Mikkola's clutches while both Vatanen and Toivonen retired soon afterwards. In order to protect Audi's manufacturer points, Gumpert ordered his drivers to hold station and Mikkola cruised to yet another 1,000 Lakes win in front of the muzzled Blomqvist and a delirious home crowd.

Audi's tally was thus bolstered and Mouton was not yet out of the game in the drivers' championship battle – although those missing points from Finland rankled. Whether by accident or design, Walter Röhrl was piling on the pressure in every way possible, looking relaxed on the Sanremo sea front before the start of the next event, declaring:

'The main thing I realised at the beginning of the year is that the challenge would come from a new technology, a new car with four-wheel drive, that shows the way into the future. Probably I would lose against it but I can't see anything bad with that.'

The inference was clear: Röhrl would not be beaten by a woman. A show of strength would be required from Audi, and Gumpert, together

with David Sutton, brought six crews to the event: Mikkola/Hertz, Mouton/Pons, Blomqvist/Cederberg and Wittmann/Diekmann with the works and Sutton cars for Cinotto/Radaelli and Demuth/Fischer.

In many respects it was too many cars for even the combined teams to cope with and repeatedly cars left service with unresolved issues or incorrect components. Despite this, and with no team orders, Blomqvist soared off into the lead to take victory from Mikkola. Mouton was fourth behind Walter Röhrl's Opel with Cinotto sixth, Wittmann crashing out early and Demuth losing his engine.

All of this put Audi in a commanding position in the manufacturers' title race, but Mouton's championship hopes were fading. She would have to beat Röhrl in both of the remaining events and hope that he had some bad luck.

Audi went to Bandama in the Ivory Coast with two heavily reinforced cars for the annual slog through Africa's roughest terrain. This time, Mikkola fell in line and drove his car as a support vehicle to Mouton, carrying Gumpert as co-driver and a number of spare parts.

Yet, while Mouton finally had the entire team behind her, news arrived 90 minutes before the start that her beloved father had died and she was forced to compete in a state of shock and grief – although she overcame it and left Röhrl standing for much of the rally.

With the end practically in sight, however, she fumbled. Delayed by wet electrics, which allowed Röhrl to close up, she put the hammer down and made one small mistake, which turned into a rally-ending accident. To this day,

the story told is that Michèle Mouton lost the world championship on the Ivory Coast Rally but, in fact, her fate had been sealed much earlier in the season. At the time of writing, in 2019, her 1982 campaign is one that no other woman has come close to equalling in the annals of world championship motor sport.

Röhrl's unexpected victory in Africa ended the drivers' title race in his favour and put Opel firmly back in with a chance of taking the manufacturers' title on the RAC Rally. As a 'blind' rally without reconnaissance passes, this was an event that Röhrl made no secret about detesting as it gave an advantage to local drivers – and meanwhile he had signed a contract with Lancia for 1983, putting its rapid little Group B car at his disposal.

It was a perfect storm for Opel chief Tony Fall, who brought cars for Henri Toivonen and new signing Ari Vatanen, both of whom loved

ABOVE LEFT Having obligingly sat behind Mikkola in Finland, Blomqvist was given free rein to win in Sanremo, with Mouton the biggest loser as Audi failed to support its only title contender. *(McKlein)*

ABOVE Learning of her father's death just before the start, Mouton drove like a woman possessed on the Ivory Coast but crashed out almost within sight of the finish. *(McKlein)*

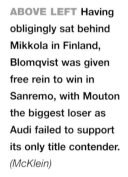

LEFT Having sealed the drivers' title in Africa, Walter Röhrl was very publicly sent home before the start of the RAC Rally – experiencing British Rail sandwiches doubtless being the final indignity. *(McKlein)*

ABOVE With Röhrl away the Quattros played – Mikkola was in his element and led Mouton home to an Audi 1-2 on the RAC Rally as the new manufacturers' champions. *(McKlein)*

BELOW Having recruited Walter Röhrl to drive its gem-like Group B car, Lancia then used every trick in the book – and wrote a few more chapters – to win the Monte Carlo Rally. *(McKlein)*

BELOW RIGHT Struggling on the salty asphalt, Mikkola sought to minimise the damage at the start of a concerted push for the drivers' world championship. *(McKlein)*

the British event. There was a late change to the entry list, however, when he sent Röhrl home in favour of Opel stalwart Jochi Kleint.

'Obviously his heart was not in it and we want the maximum performance that we can from every single member of our team,' Fall told the TV cameras at the start. 'Kleint is the other German A-seeded driver, he needs to have a good result now, this year, to actually retain his A-seeding and we think that he will be hungry enough now, as this is his last chance, to do an actual better performance than Walter Röhrl.'

It was a low blow but ultimately was rather academic. The RAC Rally belonged to Audi Sport as Mikkola drove to victory with Mouton behind him. Vatanen's car blew a head gasket, leaving Toivonen's Opel and Alén's Lancia to squabble over the last podium placing. Three

other Quattros appeared, of which Harald Demuth finished fifth in a Sutton car, young British talent Malcolm Wilson came home tenth in Audi UK's primary car and North American champion John Buffum was 12th in his Audi USA-backed Quattro. Just a few weeks later, the 1983 season would begin.

The 1983 World Rally Championship

Audi's interim Group B car was called the Quattro A1, its name used to denote the lighter aluminium engine block that nestled in a body that was outwardly similar to its Group 4 and road cars. In contrast, Lancia had built its pert little 037 Rallye to shave the limits of every regulation from the ground up; team principal Cesare Fiorio and his merry men had taken on the same determination as a team of commandos behind enemy lines.

They had an all-star driver pairing of Markku Alén in one car and Walter Röhrl in the other, but to tackle Audi would mean being open to every available tactic to achieve their objectives.

The extent to which Lancia was prepared to wage war upon the world championship was revealed in Monte Carlo when, in conditions of ice and snow, the Lancias set off wearing slick tyres. They were barely under control for the first few kilometres but then, miraculously, the roads cleared and virgin asphalt appeared beneath their wheels, as though somehow the roads from Corsica had been lifted and laid down beneath the Lancias. In some ways they had.

'Fiorio sent a few trucks with 40 tonnes of salt a week before,' Röhrl chuckled, years later. 'They have sprinkled vigorously so that the snow is gone!'

Nothing in the rules precluded teams from completely changing the road surface to suit their cars – it was simply that very few other teams would have come up with the notion. For Cesare Fiorio, however, it was all in a day's work. Not only did he have a small Italian army throwing salt down, but he also convinced the event organisers to do the same, making an elaborate case that not doing so would leave them culpable in the event of injuries to spectators, resulting from them slipping on too much ice and snow on the stages.

Throughout the event, Lancia kept a very close eye on the road conditions and had tyre barges waiting on the actual stages – ready to switch from slick to studded rubber if needed. 'If you want to compete in motor sport, you must know the rules you have to face,' Fiorio later said. 'The grey zones of the rules… and it's always a big fight but you must try to be a bit clever.'

Röhrl romped to victory in front of Alén while Blomqvist finished third for Audi in front of Mikkola. Michèle Mouton had crashed out on the 11th special stage, but at least had the consolation of not putting Fabrizia Pons in the hands of the medics this year.

Back in Ingolstadt, the limits to which Lancia was prepared to reach for victory gave pause for thought. Development of the thoroughbred Group B Quattro became all-consuming, while Audi realised that winning the drivers'

championship was, in many ways, more important than the manufacturers' title.

In 1982 nobody outside the respective boardrooms had paid much attention to the contest between Audi and Opel because they were wide-eyed at the battle between Röhrl and Mouton, with all its attendant press headlines. In 1983, therefore, Audi would go out of its way to ensure that one driver would beat Walter Röhrl and that driver would be Hannu Mikkola.

Partly to help him along in this respect, and partly to promote the new road-going model, Stig Blomqvist would compete in the Swedish Rally at the wheel of a Group A production class Audi 80 quattro, down 100 bhp for the absence of a turbo. With Lancia electing to miss Sweden, Mikkola duly took victory at the head of a 1-2-3-4 result for Audi – and the fact that Blomqvist was second overall in the 80 quattro was a jolt for everyone.

Portugal came next and with it the Lancias returned to battle. The Quattros were on their mettle and finished with Mikkola winning from Mouton. Next came the Safari Rally and Lancia again chose to skip an event for which its little coupés were ill-suited but Audi made its debut on the event. An extraordinary game of long-distance snakes and ladders ensued in which all of the lead contenders shone, struck problems and fell back before recovering once again. When the last stage was over, Ari Vatanen won for Opel with Mikkola and Mouton right behind them.

Gumpert's team travelled to Corsica for its bogey event with two of the heavily revised Audi

Quattro A2 cars for Mikkola and Mouton. The second aluminium engine had a smaller swept volume than other Quattros, with 2,110cc. This dropped the Quattro down into the 'below 3-litre class' when multiplied by 1.4 to compensate for the turbo. But nobody specified the size of the turbo (or intercooler), which had grown significantly, with Audi confirming that 400 bhp had been seen from the 'baby' engine.

This much power was allied to a more advanced and lightweight construction (see Chapter 4), evidenced from the roadside by a second air intake in front of the rear wheels – this one for cooling the rear differential. Despite the obvious enhancements to its design, teething problems prevented either of the Quattro A2s from reaching the finish, handing Lancia a 1-2-3-4 result with Alén beating Röhrl.

Next came the Acropolis, and Audi could at least hope that the Lancias would struggle to survive the brutal nature of the Greek stages. When it came to it, Mikkola's car went out after the boot lid flew off on a night stage and pulled the oil reservoir out with it, while Mouton rolled her A2 into a ball. Stig Blomqvist was on hand with a third example and set a blistering string of stage wins, but could finish no higher than third behind the Lancias of Röhrl and Alén.

The championship was at boiling point in New Zealand, and Audi Sport decided to enter Blomqvist in a third car once again. The entry was late but accepted by the organisers – but not so by Lancia, who protested and had the Swede pulled out of the rally while he was running in second place. Röhrl took the win and both Mouton and Mikkola suffered engine failures – Mikkola's resulting in a fire which, eagle-eyed observers noted, was the tenth conflagration of the Quattro's World Rally Championship career.

Argentina followed, returning to the calendar with a rugged route around the Andes. Finally, the Audi Quattro A2s held together and performed as planned, with Mikkola taking victory from Blomqvist, dutifully guarding the team leader's tail, with Mouton third and guest driver Shekhar Mehta ending up fourth.

In Finland for the 1,000 Lakes, Hannu Mikkola was in trouble early on. He lost the front differential on his first major jump and then he lost his turbo after the engine mounts broke over another. 'I always remember it was an 85km [53 mile] road section and I knew it takes 40 minutes and I knew there would be a lot of police,' Mikkola recalled later.

'So I said to Arne "Give me the map" and I looked at another road on the side and I went flat out. I got there on time and they changed the engine mount.'

The fired-up Finn was delayed again by a loose turbo but by the final morning was back in second place with 24 seconds being the deficit to Blomqvist – and 20 miles [32km] of competitive rally remaining to him. As the field mustered at the stage start, Roland Gumpert reminded Blomqvist in no uncertain terms what was expected of him, and Mikkola duly won that last stage by 45 seconds.

Audi would have to beat Lancia heavily in Sanremo to stand a chance of winning the manufacturers' title, while a Lancia win would give it to the Italians on home soil. Small wonder that it was a 'maximum effort' from Cesare Fiorio's men, who tried to repeat their trick of creating optimum road conditions by driving vans over the gravel stages with brooms underneath that swept loose gravel away.

That ploy failed, but in the end they didn't need it. Audi Sport entered four Quattros for Mikkola/Hertz, Mouton/Pons, Blomqvist/ Cederberg and French asphalt rally hero Bernard Darniche with co-driver Alain Mahé. Mouton was the highest-placed finisher in seventh, Darniche was ninth, Blomqvist crashed heavily and Mikkola's car burned down to the ground. The 1983 manufacturers' title belonged to Lancia, which ended with Alén winning from Röhrl and third driver Attilio Bettega, but although Röhrl still had a mathematical chance of beating Mikkola to the drivers' title he had no intention of competing in the Ivory Coast or RAC Rallies.

ABOVE Mikkola was single-minded in his pursuit of victory at home in Finland. *(McKlein)*

While Lancia celebrated, Röhrl wandered over to the Audi service area and sought out his rival. 'I said "Hannu, enjoy it! You are world champion, I am happy, it is beautiful!"'

On the Ivory Coast, Audi sent one car for Mikkola with promising young Finnish driver Lasse Lampi acting as his teammate and support vehicle. Some locals were rather upset about the rally interrupting their peace and quiet so they laid a tree in the road, which Mikkola hit, bending the shell and handing the initiative to his old teammate Björn Waldegård in a Toyota. Second place was sufficient to mean that even if Röhrl did appear in Britain, he could only tie on points at best.

ABOVE Audi's dreams of the manufacturers' title ended in ignominy on the Sanremo, with Lancia claiming four of the top five places. This is the remains of Mikkola's car. *(McKlein)*

ABOVE Walter Röhrl's
first appearance in
an Audi, on a national
event in Germany,
ended with a fearsome
accident from which
he and co-driver
Christian Geistdörfer
were lucky to escape.
(McKlein)

BELOW Another
Audi Quattro win on
the RAC Rally – this
time Stig Blomqvist
claiming the honours
in Audi UK's entry
beating Mikkola's
factory car. *(McKlein)*

In the end, Röhrl did not appear. A week before the RAC Rally, the Bavarian had gone out and quietly driven in a domestic German rally at the start of his new job – as an Audi Sport driver. He discovered that the Quattro was a very different beast in comparison with the Lancia and understeered into some trees. He had much to learn if finally getting his hands on a four-wheel-drive car was going to live up to expectations.

Meanwhile in Britain, Mikkola and Mouton appeared for the works team with Lasse Lampi in his Finnish championship car from David Sutton, along with fellow Finnish Quattro drivers Antero Laine and Jouko Saarinen in their own cars. American champion John Buffum returned, British ace Darryl Weidner appeared with an ex-Sutton car and Stig Blomqvist was in the Audi Sport UK Quattro A2, with which he had won the 1983 British championship.

With the drivers' title settled, no team orders

were enforced and Blomqvist led from the start. Mikkola lost a wheel in his pursuit but fought back from 20th to second place at the finish, happy to share the podium and accept the cheers of British fans who, after so many years, claimed both crews as their own.

The 1984 World Rally Championship

Three Audi Quattro A2 cars were entered for the 1984 Monte Carlo Rally by the works team for Walter Röhrl/Christian Geistdörfer, Stig Blomqvist/Björn Cederberg and Hannu Mikkola/Arne Hertz. All three were resplendent in a new livery after the addition of sponsorship from the HB brand of tobacco. Also joining the squad was the Audi 80 quattro, which would be crewed by Bernard Darniche/Alain Mahé in the hope of winning Group A honours.

The drivers were seeded according to their results the previous year, so Röhrl was number 1, Mikkola number 4 and Blomqvist number 7. For the first time since 1981 the route was blanketed with snow, and the stage seemed set for a Quattro whitewash.

Blomqvist took a good lead early on and, having worked relentlessly to master the Quattro and its preferred left-foot braking technique, Röhrl was infuriated by losing time to the Swede on every stage. Röhrl recalled:

'Stig had done the tyre testing and I had done suspension testing. At the service the team said: "OK, the next stage is 80% wet snow. Stig and Hannu said we must use tyre number four." OK, we'll put all three cars on number four. After the stage, I was thinking I was quick, but Stig was 30 seconds faster. Oh Mamma Mia!

'The second stage was a long one, over three Cols – around 50km [31 miles]. The same situation, talking tyres and saying that all three cars would be on the same. And then I said to Christian "ask on the radio what Stig's time is". He was 1min 34sec faster than me. I was thinking I should just stop and kill myself!

'We had a long road section to get to the next service. One of my best friends was spectating on the second stage and he took a more direct route to the service. I got out of the car and he said, "You are the greatest!"

'Yeah, sure – but I'm one and a half minutes slower than Stig. He said: "On the stage, I watched you. You looked so much faster than anybody else…"

'I had a good connection with one mechanic – because I was new to the team. I said: "Hans, if you lie I will kill you! What's happened here?" He said: "Once you start, the others change tyres." Before the next stage I said to the team chief: "Listen. If this happens once more I'm going to the next cliff and pushing the car off it." On the next stage I was one minute faster, on the same tyres as the others!'

With the playing field thus levelled, Röhrl swept past Blomqvist to head an Audi 1-2-3, which in turn completed a remarkable run of four consecutive Monte Carlo wins in four different cars for the Bavarian. Audi's joy was completed when Darniche drove into Monaco in seventh place overall to win Group A by more than 25 minutes.

For Walter Röhrl, honour was satisfied. Thus the die was cast: Blomqvist would drive on all events, with the rest of the team acting on a rotation basis to help deliver the manufacturers' title and support their Swedish colleague's championship bid.

Audi scored another 1-2-3 in Sweden, with Blomqvist winning from Michèle Mouton and guest driver Per Eklund third. A maximum-effort raid on Portugal followed, with Blomqvist, Röhrl and Mikkola being joined by a fourth car for Audi's South African champion Sarel van der Merwe.

Lancias held sway on the asphalt stages but then Blomqvist broke a suspension mount and

lost nine minutes. In his hurry to regain the time, he crashed out – as did van der Merwe. Röhrl also crashed but continued in order to play a little game with his old teammates at Lancia.

Only Mikkola was in a position to bring home the win, but the Lancias were proving too fast and too reliable to guarantee it. To aid Mikkola's cause, Röhrl therefore clocked in ahead of his teammate at the start of every stage, allowing Mikkola much better visibility as the dust thrown up by the Lancias had twice as long to settle. After 700 miles (1,126km), Mikkola beat Markku Alén by just 27 seconds.

ABOVE Tyres were the main talking point at Audi in the early stages of the 1984 Monte Carlo Rally – with Walter Röhrl being left fuming by the in-house gamesmanship. *(McKlein)*

BELOW LEFT After threatening to push his car into a ravine, Röhrl was given the same tyres as his team mates and duly hurled his Quattro on to Audi's first win on the event – and his fourth consecutive win with four different manufacturers. *(McKlein)*

BELOW Local hero Per Eklund joined Audi's squad in Sweden, completing a second 1-2-3 result for the Quattro in successive rallies. *(McKlein)*

Röhrl had no interest in the Safari Rally so the old guard of Blomqvist, Mikkola, Mouton and Wittmann set out for Kenya. Blomqvist and Mouton retired with engine problems but Mikkola survived several similar engine scares to finish third, with Wittmann sixth.

Next came the Tour de Corse but for the first time Audi felt a glimmer of hope going into the rally, as this would be the debut of its short wheelbase car, the Audi Sport quattro, complete with the new 20-valve, 420 horsepower engine and a 6-speed gearbox. Alongside it stood the new four-wheel-drive contender from Peugeot: the mid-engined 205 Turbo 16, driven by Ari Vatanen/Terry Harryman in the lead car and supported by Jean-Pierre Nicolas/Charley Pasquier in the second entry.

The Sport quattros made wild progress around the French island, sliding luridly at every opportunity. They were closer to the Lancias than the old long-wheelbase cars had been – but in turn the Lancias were being left for dead by Vatanen's astonishing new Peugeot. Röhrl went out with engine failure and then Vatanen crashed ferociously, putting the Lancias of Alén and Miki Biasion into the top positions. Blomqvist finished fifth, 21 minutes behind the winner.

After Röhrl had suffered a repeat of their engine problems in the Sport quattro while testing on the Metz Rallye Stein in Germany, Blomqvist elected to drive the old 10-valve Quattro A2 on the Acropolis Rally – as did Hannu Mikkola. The new cars were entered for Röhrl and Michèle Mouton, while John Buffum had a Sutton-prepared A2 with Fred Gallagher as his co-driver.

Once again, Vatanen took the early lead but there would be no denying Audi this time. Although both of the Sport quattros retired with mechanical issues, the older cars finished first (Blomqvist), second (Mikkola) and fifth (Buffum).

None of the short wheelbase cars made the long trek to New Zealand. Instead four A2s made the journey for Blomqvist, Mikkola, Röhrl and Wittmann. Blomqvist won once again, with Mikkola rolling and the car catching fire, but it was doused soon enough for him to repair it and continue. Neither Röhrl nor Wittmann had such luck and fell foul of mechanical failures.

The Stig and Hannu show meanwhile arrived in Argentina where they were joined by national rally legend Jorge Recalde and fellow countryman Rubén Luis de Palma. For the third time in the season it was an Audi 1-2-3 with Mikkola riding shotgun to Blomqvist – although the crowd's biggest cheers were reserved for Recalde's fine third place.

Next came the 1,000 Lakes and another three-car squad left Ingolstadt for Jyväskylä with a 10-valve Quattro A2 for Blomqvist and a brace of 20-valve Audi Sport quattros for Mikkola and Mouton. Both of the short wheelbase cars went out – Mouton crashing heavily and Mikkola breaking the steering on a jump. Blomqvist found that the old engine was at a significant disadvantage and was powerless to hold back the Lancias, which were in turn unable to hold on to Ari Vatanen in the remarkable little Peugeot, who took the victory.

With the drivers' title almost sealed in his favour, Blomqvist acquiesced and took a Sport quattro to Sanremo, alongside the sister car of Walter Röhrl, after an intensive few weeks of testing for the German. Ferdinand Piëch arrived to see how progress was going, and witnessed the Swede's car blowing its engine early in the running, which at least gave Röhrl the

opportunity to go at full tilt, holding the same pace as Vatanen's Peugeot until a rare error triggered a sizeable accident.

Despite Audi failing to score in Italy, the titles were still all-but out of reach for Lancia and only Audi made the trip to the Ivory Coast out of the major European squads, where Blomqvist's Audi Sport quattro and Mikkola's A2 went up against the local specialists of Nissan and Toyota. The pair simply drove away and Blomqvist scored the Sport quattro's first win to seal both championships. Not only that, but it was Audi's 22nd world championship win since 1981, making it the most successful manufacturer in history.

It had been Audi's most convincing season to date: its most co-ordinated and its most successful. Yet for all that, there were still huge reservations about the reliability and handling of the stumpy Sport quattro and its mighty

ABOVE LEFT New star rising: the Peugeot 205 Turbo 16 was devastatingly fast on asphalt and gravel alike. Even as the team seemed assured of winning both the drivers' and manufacturers' titles, it appeared that the era of the Quattro was coming to a close. *(McKlein)*

ABOVE Ferdinand Piëch (left) came to Sanremo to see his team stride towards championship success in the new Sport quattros. Blomqvist's engine blew and Röhrl crashed. *(McKlein)*

LEFT Victory in the Ivory Coast made Stig Blomqvist world champion and made Audi the most successful manufacturer in world championship history. It was to be the only victory for the Sport quattro in its original form. *(McKlein)*

ABOVE Audi's run of success on the RAC Rally ended abruptly in 1984, with Ari Vatanen's Peugeot dominant and Mouton (pictured) an unhappy fourth in the Sport quattro. *(McKlein)*

Chester to flag the event away and drive a Land Rover at improbable speed to entertain the masses. Audi UK decided to capitalise on the most successful season in the sport and funded the appearance of Michèle Mouton in an Audi Sport quattro as well as covering Hannu Mikkola's fee to drive its own David Sutton-built Quattro A2.

After a hugely successful season that included his first European win in Cyprus, John Buffum returned for another RAC while Malcolm Wilson's ex-Sutton car completed a very strong line-up. Most of the major opposition was two-wheel-drive machinery and the weather had been particularly foul but then there was the solo Peugeot 205 T16 of Ari Vatanen and Terry Harryman – and the little Peugeot simply danced away from the Audis.

Just like Mikkola two years earlier, Vatanen had time enough in hand to crash and repair the car before shooting back into the lead on the final leg. All of the Quattros hit mechanical problems along the way and ran as a pack until Wilson and Buffum both went out. Mikkola finished second and Mouton fourth, but it was very clear that neither of the current Quattros could match the Peugeot on either loose or paved surfaces.

Walter Röhrl cancelled Christmas. He had some testing to do.

BELOW Weeks of pre-event testing and his cast iron will saw Walter Röhrl come close to beating Vatanen's Peugeot on the 1985 Monte Carlo Rally. But not close enough. *(McKlein)*

but frail engine. Moreover, the Group B era was really starting to hit its stride and Audi was swimming against the tide of mid-engined thoroughbred competition cars that was rising up to meet them.

Nowhere was Audi's tenuous grip on the series more evident than on the season-ending RAC Rally. Audi decided to save some money and pulled Stig Blomqvist's entry shortly before the event got started – although he was in

The 1985 FIA World Rally Championship

Quality not quantity marked the start of the 1985 season. Lancia was busy working on a four-wheel-drive replacement for the 037 Rallye so it sent just one car to open its account in Monte Carlo, to be driven by Henri Toivonen. A second car was entered for works driver Miki Biasion by the second-string Jolly Club. Audi sent two Sport quattros upon which to pin its hopes of victory, entered for Blomqvist/ Cederberg and Röhrl/Geistdörfer.

The pre-event favourites were three works Peugeot 205 T16s for Vatanen/Harryman, Timo Salonen/Seppo Harjanne and Bruno Saby/ Jean-François Fauchille, but Röhrl was not to be intimidated on his most cherished event. His weeks of testing delivered good speed in the opening stages while Vatanen went off, hitting three spectators and causing one broken leg. All parties recovered but then the usually unflappable Harryman made an error and clocked them in to a time control four minutes early, their penalty handing the lead to Röhrl by almost five minutes with just under 400km (250 miles) of timed stages to run.

The decider would be the Col de St Raphael stage, which started uphill for 12km (7.5 miles) of thick snow and ice before a 30km (19 mile) run on bone-dry asphalt. Röhrl stayed on intermediate tyres while Vatanen switched to studs and pulled out a lead of more than six minutes, passing Röhrl in the ascent, and then holding on bravely to the finish. For the first time in the 1980s, Röhrl was beaten in Monte Carlo.

Vatanen won again in Sweden, this time with the Sport quattro of Blomqvist trailing him home. Timo Salonen beat the Sport quattros in Portugal and on the Safari both Mikkola and Blomqvist went out with engine problems. It was Audi's worst start to any season and the next event would be Corsica. To complicate life further, Ferdinand Piëch would be in attendance.

Roland Gumpert had proposed a radically different version of the Sport quattro, an upgraded car with better aerodynamics and weight distribution, together with more power. Audi did not like it because it looked too different to its showroom products but, with no victories on the horizon, it was reluctantly built. The new

car was not ready for Corsica, however, so Röhrl set to work with a regular Sport quattro.

In Corsica, a catastrophic accident befell the Lancia 037 of Attilio Bettega, and the popular Italian was killed. For once the Peugeots were not on form, Salonen's electrics giving up and Vatanen crashing, but Röhrl's brakes could not take the strain and he also retired, leaving Jean Ragnotti as the unlikely winner in his Renault – and leaving Gumpert facing a deeply uncomfortable conversation with Piëch.

Salonen won again on the Acropolis and in New Zealand, with Röhrl, Blomqvist and Mikkola left to scrap over the crumbs. There was a break in the World Rally Championship calendar during July but Audi was working furiously as it sent the new car, the Audi Sport quattro S1, to tackle the Olympus Rally in Washington State as its first competitive outing. Hannu Mikkola won, with John Buffum's Quattro A1 a distant second.

The same car then travelled back across

TOP After Monte Carlo, the Sport quattros could offer little resistance to Peugeot on any surface. Here Röhrl presses on fruitlessly in Portugal. *(McKlein)*

ABOVE Ferdinand Piëch attended the Tour de Corse in 1985. Lancia driver Attilio Bettega was killed and Röhrl was withdrawn after brake failure. *(McKlein)*

LEFT The mighty Audi Sport quattro S1 got its world championship debut in Argentina – Blomqvist rearranging its aerodynamics and going out with engine failure. *(McKlein)*

BELOW Weeks of testing in Sanremo saw Röhrl and the S1 honed to perfection. He would stand alone against the mid-engined cars in Italy. *(McKlein)*

BELOW RIGHT In one of the all-time great world championship drives, Röhrl pulled away from the nimbler cars through a combination of horsepower and willpower. *(McKlein)*

the Atlantic to Northern Ireland and the Ulster Rally, where Michèle Mouton prepared to make its asphalt debut. Still on the soft gravel setup used in America, she managed to set the fastest time on Stage 1 but then a leak in the turbo caused her to pull out rather than break the 510 horsepower, 20-valve screamer.

In the same week, final preparations were underway for the Audi Sport quattro S1 to make its world championship debut in Argentina. Stig Blomqvist and Björn Cederberg crewed the lone works entry, although Austrian privateer Wilfried Wiedner took his ex-works Quattro A2 along. Blomqvist's engine failed but Wiedner finished second to Salonen's Peugeot, in a rally remembered for the life-threatening injuries suffered by Ari Vatanen when his Peugeot hit a dip in the road and rolled end-over-end.

Three weeks later, in Finland, Blomqvist and Mikkola drove a pair of S1s on the 1,000 Lakes. Mikkola's engine failed after recovering from earlier mechanical problems. Blomqvist's

car was in better health but he had to settle for second place behind Salonen's Peugeot.

Back in Ingolstadt, Walter Röhrl had been putting his weight behind the S1 development programme and then spent three weeks in the car testing around Sanremo. It was a quite incomprehensible effort but Audi Sport had to show something in return for the vast outlay that had been spent on developing the new car. Only Röhrl was present for the team in Italy – but in the end that's all they needed.

Initially the Lancias again led on the asphalt stages but the Bavarian was right with them. When they hit the gravel he pounced, setting 28 fastest stage times to build a lead that could not be challenged, even by Salonen. It was a lavish and unsustainable way to go rallying, but at least the Audi Sport quattro S1 had this one world championship victory to its name.

A pair of the earlier Sport quattros was sent over to Africa for the Ivory Coast Rally – Michèle Mouton driving the lead car with Arne Hertz alongside her, while Franz Braun and Arwed Fischer drove a sister car as the flying service truck. When Mouton's car dropped out of the lead battle with serious engine problems the chase car found her and repairs were made out in the bush.

After the repair stop, Mouton took off at full

speed but there were rumours circulating that she was in fact driving the chase car, which had been hurriedly fitted with the doors and bonnet from her own car. Photographs taken certainly show that the fit and finish was a little different to how she had left the start ramp, but the car was inspected by scrutineers and no concerns were raised.

In a rather tense atmosphere, Mouton's charge was again blunted by mechanical trouble and in the end her car was withdrawn. To this day, arguments rage over what happened, but the only comment given to this author by a member of the team was that 'Gumpert got thrown under a bus'.

The season ended traditionally in Britain with the RAC Rally. A pair of Audi Sport quattro S1s departed Ingolstadt – a standard car for Hannu Mikkola/Arne Hertz and a very special machine destined for Walter Röhrl. One of the many projects that had preoccupied Röhrl in his protracted absences from competition in 1985 was fitting Porsche's PDK transmission to the Audi.

The seamless gearchanges of the PDK were astonishing, as were the speeds it allowed Röhrl to reach, but he had no desire at all to compete in the RAC Rally and it took a fair amount of leverage within Audi to encourage him. He would be partnered with British co-driver Phil Short, which mollified the truculent star somewhat to have some local knowledge in the cockpit.

The RAC Rally also marked the World Rally Championship debut of new Group B weaponry – the Lancia Delta S4 and Austin Rover's MG Metro 6R4.

The Lancia was mid-engined, four-wheel drive and its engine was both supercharged and turbocharged to give optimum power just shy of 500 bhp and superior throttle response. Two cars arrived for Henri Toivonen/Neil Wilson and Markku Alén/Ilkka Kivimäki. In contrast to all the other Group B cars, the Metro did not have a turbo but instead a bespoke 3-litre V6 racing engine good for 400 bhp with no lag at all and local hero Tony Pond at the wheel, co-driven by Rob Arthur.

It produced a furious opening leg from which Röhrl crashed out violently while pursuing the Peugeots and Lancias. Mikkola, the old master of the RAC, managed to get the standard S1 singing and took the lead but then the advanced electronics of the 20-valve engine management system began to go haywire.

ABOVE LEFT The 1985 Ivory Coast Rally effectively ended the tenure of Roland Gumpert as team principal (centre), and the tale of Michèle Mouton and these two Sport quattros remains a hot one among rally fans. *(McKlein)*

ABOVE Porsche's PDK transmission startled onlookers in the car driven by Walter Röhrl and Phil Short until a gigantic accident ended their RAC Rally. *(McKlein)*

RIGHT The humble little Austin Metro was reborn as the 6R4 and with the host nation willing it onward, Tony Pond secured third on the RAC Rally. *(McKlein)*

ABOVE On their world championship debut, the Lancia Delta S4s of Markku Alèn and Henri Toivonen crushed all opposition on the RAC Rally and aimed high for 1986. *(McKlein)*

departure was that of Roland Gumpert, who had masterminded all of Audi's title-winning successes but upon whom responsibility had fallen both for Röhrl's abject Corsican performance and the potential damage to Audi's reputation that would have come from any cheating in the Ivory Coast. More sad days were too soon to follow.

The 1986 World Rally Championship

In 1980, when the rules were agreed, Group B was never intended to create 500+ horsepower four-wheel-drive projectiles with advanced aerodynamics. The rules had worked in that they created an unprecedented spectacle and brought millions of people around the world to stand on the special stages and urge the cars on – but the stakes were now incredibly high for crews, spectators and the sport as a whole.

FISA and the manufacturers had broadly agreed a revised package, Group S, for 1987 onwards. The existing cars could be modified and, by dropping the requirement to build 200 road-going examples, the extravagant costs could be reduced. They would look even more insane but their performance would be moderated and many safety features not present on the current cars would be mandated.

Meanwhile, the 1986 season got underway in Monte Carlo and Audi Sport fielded two S1s for Röhrl and Mikkola against the Peugeot 205 T16s, the Lancia Delta S4s and the MG Metro 6R4s. Their new manager was a man called Herwart Kreiner, who was ill at ease with rallying.

BELOW The manic intensity that surrounded rallies continued to swell in 1986 with bigger and bigger crowds becoming ever-more unruly. Here Röhrl threads the needle in Monte Carlo. *(McKlein)*

BELOW RIGHT Henri Toivonen bent the chassis of his Lancia after hitting a spectator's car on the Monte. He still trounced all comers. *(McKlein)*

Unlike an old carburettor car, this sort of job couldn't be fixed at the roadside, and thus the screaming S1 fell silent.

The Peugeots also went out, which left Lancia rather stunned, holding the top two places on their car's debut and fending off a determined attack from Pond's raucous Metro. In the end the victory went to Toivonen, with Alèn a minute behind and Pond in third. Per Eklund saved some pride for Audi by finishing fourth in a private Quattro A2.

An era ended for Audi Sport in the wintry wet and cold of northern England. Stig Blomqvist would leave the team for a long-term deal with Ford. Michèle Mouton also left to spearhead Peugeot's assault on the German national championship. The other major

Röhrl challenged hard but road salt got into the electronics and gave him a power-sapping misfire that could not be fixed. Mikkola had an untroubled run but could only hope for misfortune to hit the Lancias and Peugeots – which it did, but not enough. Henri Toivonen collided with a spectator's car but still managed to win.

The team then decided to miss the Swedish Rally, at which Ford debuted its new mid-engined RS200, but a single car was entered for Röhrl in Portugal. The event got underway but was still in its early asphalt stages when the privately entered RS200 of local ace Joaquim Santos went off and into the crowd, killing as many as ten people. In extraordinary scenes, the drivers of the works cars refused to go on with the rally, as no assurances on controlling the crowds could be given by event organisers.

Audi stepped back in the wake of the tragedy, releasing a statement that it was assessing all options, including a mid-engined car, for future competition. Immediately this position was contradicted by Ferdinand Piëch who, in a rare interview, criticised FISA for allowing rally cars to become divorced from showroom product and expressed interest in touring car racing. Meanwhile, without Audi, the fateful Tour de Corse played out in which Henri Toivonen and co-driver Sergio Cresto died as their Lancia burned in a ravine.

A crisis meeting was held in Paris in the days that followed, at which Audi insisted that Group B could continue if the event organisers would enforce better crowd control and FISA demanded basic safety measures such as crash testing of safety structures, that flammable composite materials were banned and that fuel tanks were repositioned. No such commitments were gained and less than a week later, Audi AG issued another statement to announce its withdrawal from the 1986 World Rally Championship.

Two weeks later, in the German national championship, former F1 star Marc Surer was competing for victory in a Ford RS200 against the Peugeot 205 T16 of Michèle Mouton. Going through a fast right-hander the car ran wide and struck a tree, breaking in half and bursting into flames. Surer was thrown out of the wreck and was critically injured but his co-driver, Michel Wyder, was trapped in the inferno and died.

Group S was cancelled with immediate effect and Group B was bundled out of the door as fast as possible.

Quattros would continue to appear in the world championship until the end of the season, entered by David Sutton and numerous privateers. The honour of the last competitive start in the series fell to John Buffum at the season-ending Olympus Rally, the USA's debut as a host, in which he finished third.

The legacy of the Audi Quattro remained undiminished, however. In 1987, production-based Group A regulations became the senior category in the sport, and every successful car of the era needed both four-wheel drive and a turbocharger. That same formula has held true from the Monte Carlo Rally of 1981 until the present day, and among millions of people the world over there is still nothing to compare with the sight and sound of a five-cylinder Audi at full speed, its crews forever in the top echelons of the sport's heroes. Long may they be so.

ABOVE The long-predicted carnage occurred when a new Ford RS200 swerved to avoid one errant fan and hit more than 30 others on the Portugal Rally. The works drivers refused to continue and so ended an era. *(McKlein)*

BELOW Quattros continued to appear throughout the 1986 season, even after the works team had withdrawn. Here Harald Demuth drives the Audi UK Sport quattro on the RAC Rally. *(McKlein)*

Chapter Three

The Audi Quattro drivers

Across the multitude of championships contested by the Audi Quattro in Europe, America, Africa and Scandinavia, a small army of extremely talented stars took their turns at the wheel – and won significant honours. Many of them will be met in the remainder of this book, but in the pantheon of the FIA World Rally Championship there was a core of just four upon whose results the image of Audi around the world was forged. These are their stories.

OPPOSITE Life in a rally team brings together big personalities who eat, sleep and travel the world together – usually in a close-knit team. *(McKlein)*

RIGHT Hannu Mikkola
led the second wave
of Finnish talent
to reach the world
championship, seen
here in his first full
season with Ford in
1969. (McKlein)

Hannu Mikkola

Born:
24 May 1942, Joensuu, Finland
World Rally Championship Victories:
18 (9 with Audi)
World Rally Championship Titles:
1983 (Audi)

Finland grew famous as the homeland of professional rally superstars in the early 1960s. The French and Italians were fast on tarmac and the British were fast on gravel but the Finns were fast everywhere as they preached the gospel of left-foot braking and the Scandinavian flick, while the sport entered a new and exciting professional era.

After Rauno Aaltonen and Timo Mäkinen first shook up the establishment in their Mini-Coopers, Peter Ashcroft of Ford's works rally management discovered a rapid youngster called Hannu Mikkola. With Ford behind him, Mikkola won the 1968 1,000 Lakes at the start of an unbroken three-year run of success on the event.

It also became apparent that Mikkola had an unusual degree of mechanical sympathy. In 1970, Ford entered a fleet of Escorts in the 16,000-mile (25,750km) World Cup Rally from London to Mexico and this became Mikkola's first landmark victory.

It would be followed by another marathon win for Ford when, in 1972, Mikkola became the first international driver to win the Safari Rally. He remained part of Ford's squad in the earliest seasons of the world championship, but then he and the team's management grew tired of one another and they parted company at the end of 1974.

For the rest of the decade, Mikkola was a gun for hire – and a popular one at that. He scored more world championship wins for Peugeot and Toyota, became involved in Mercedes' programme of long-distance events and would return sporadically to Ford, either in works cars or those of David Sutton, missing out on the inaugural drivers' world championship title in 1979 by a solitary point – at which moment Jürgen Stockmar picked up the telephone. Soon, Mikkola was committed to making the Quattro a contender in rallying, with 60 days of testing in 1980 to sort its new and occasionally unnerving habits.

'I could drive it faster than the Escort immediately on the wide roads, but when it was on the narrow road I never really knew within half a metre where it goes!' he recalled. 'It was pulling and it was very unstable, with the limited slip diffs and all that… We realised that the front wheels were moving and all that, and when we got that right we went to Portugal to the Algarve Rally as the Zero car.'

Mikkola's legendary half-hour 'victory' in the course car set the tone for the Quattro's early years, although so too did its mechanical frailties of which the Finn was forced to bear the brunt. Although frustrating for him at the time, today he recognises that the furious pace of developing the car and technology while in competition meant that the early Quattro was always exposed.

'…It was partly that when we got something reliable on the car we were testing the next new part. It was too hectic and at times we were entering five cars in one rally, so sometimes I felt that quantity was more important than quality,' he said.

Such has always been the conundrum facing motor sport programmes that are owned by marketing teams, with their need to win hearts and minds. Undoubtedly the teammate with whom Mikkola had the best relationship was Michèle Mouton, although her marketability was a major factor in her signing.

Mikkola remembered: 'The last question

LEFT A seasoned
professional by the
time Audi recruited
him, among
Mikkola's proudest
achievements with
Audi was to become
the first non-Swede to
conquer the Swedish
Rally. *(McKlein)*

Michèle asked when they were discussing about the contract was: "Are you hiring me as a rally driver or as a woman?" They were clever enough to say: "As a rally driver," so Michèle said: "Okay, I sign it."'

Although Mikkola took responsibility for the setup of Mouton's car alongside his own, his admiration for her speed and ability is undimmed. 'She should have been world champion in '82 but the team just blew it,' he said.

Audi Sport closed ranks around Mikkola in 1983 to ensure that he achieved the recognition that all the hard work in developing the car – quite aside from his own formidable talent – so richly deserved. 'It was satisfaction, because I'd already decided that after '84 I wouldn't do that kind of programme again.'

The Quattro continued to evolve and Mikkola remained at the forefront of the programme throughout the Group B era, culminating in the mighty bewinged S1 – a car of which Mikkola remains inordinately fond, despite its relatively modest success.

'We did all the testing for suspension and wings and all that and on one test road there, at the same time they were doing a Formula 1 race and it was exactly the same length [of road] as this Formula 1 race,' he beamed. 'We were testing on this gravel road and we were just four seconds slower than their lap times so we said it's really quite fast!'

Mikkola would remain with Audi in 1987 as

it campaigned in Group A with the 80 quattro, coupé quattro and 200 quattro, with which he claimed Audi's last win at world championship level on the Safari Rally. He then moved to Mazda in 1988 for four partial seasons but by then the sport was in a new era and eventually he stepped aside.

However, the old spirit never changes in rally drivers – and in 2005 the London–Mexico Rally was run again for historic cars, from which Mikkola emerged victorious in a Ford Escort, 35 years after his first win. He has also long made himself available for Audi whenever the old cars are wheeled out and journalists wish to be captivated by the Quattro once again. Once a rally driver: always a rally driver – and Mikkola was always one of the greatest.

BELOW Trust and
respect in each other's
abilities lay at the
heart of a supremely
happy partnership
between Mikkola
and Michèle Mouton.
(McKlein)

Michèle Mouton

Born:
23 June 1951, Grasse, France
World Rally Championship Victories:
4 (all with Audi)
Best World Rally Championship Position:
Second, 1982 (Audi)

For a girl whose parents supplied the world-famous local perfume industry with roses and jasmine, Michèle Mouton was something of a tomboy, whose love of cars saw her take to the wheel of her father's Citroën 2CV at the age of 14. She was a keen skier and a good dancer but ended up studying law and working as a trainee nurse until she discovered rallying.

'A friend was driving at amateur level,' she said. 'I went to watch him in Corsica and he didn't get on with his co-driver so he asked me. It was pure chance.'

Realising that this was what she really wanted from life, her father's counsel was not to rely on someone else's performance to make a career of it – she should take the wheel herself. He bought her an Alpine-Renault A110 with the promise that if, after a year, she had not made a

mark then she would go back to her studies.

Mouton duly claimed both the French GT class and Ladies' Championship, winning support from Renault and Elf that kept her away from the law books and carried her to the 1975 Le Mans 24 Hours, where she won her class in the endurance racing classic. As Renault's priorities shifted, Mouton moved to Fiat, where she became a seasoned ace on European asphalt events before Audi called her, out of the blue, and asked how she would feel about a full World Rally Championship programme alongside Hannu Mikkola.

Her cold and wintry first test in the car was a long way from the sun-soaked asphalt of the Côte d'Azur upon which she had carved her reputation, and the Audi Quattro was a car whose physical bulk had left even Mikkola wondering how it would work out. For a young woman whose career had been spent driving svelte Alpines and Lancias, her new mount was a very different proposition entirely.

'You get used, after a few kilometres, you get used to the car you have to drive… I mean you don't get any choice!' she laughed. 'You have to drive the car. The first time you go with four-wheel drive of course it was a little bit surprising, but it was on snow and we were with the normal tyres and we could do what we were doing with the snow tyres with the other cars so it was, you know, unbelievable. You had to get used to that, I had to get used to the left-foot braking… all that was news to me.'

Mouton herself, meanwhile, was news to the rest of the world. There were many sceptics who thought that she was there as a stunt (and that there were other drivers more deserving of a works seat). There was also a prevailing chauvinism that believed that women in motor sport served one purpose… and it was not driving. After spending the better part of a decade in the service parks of Europe, however, she was perfectly well used to dealing with the level of fascination that attended her every move.

'It's true that at that point, the fact that I was a woman was a point that made the fans wanted to come and see me more closer and everything,' she said. 'And touch me!

'I remember forever one guy opened the door to touch me when the [official] was counting three-two-one… just to go! I mean, it

BELOW Michèle Mouton was a formidable competitor for Alpine in the 1970s, hurling her nimble little coupé around the French and European championship stages.
(McKlein)

was difficult but in another way of course I was trying to understand also that it was the normal way for them and we have the chance to have a sport where the people can be so close to the driver.'

Nobody was exempt from Mouton-mania, least of all the press. Across Europe she gathered ever-more elaborate nicknames like 'the black tigress' and 'the French volcano' while in Britain every TV commentator's work was drenched with the sort of descriptive prose normally reserved for beauty pageants.

'I would hate it when the journalist would come to me at the end of a rally and say, "Can you smile?" I would say "OK, you go and find Blomqvist or Mikkola, ask them to smile and then you come back to me."'

In the Quattro's first season, Mouton gained extra mileage thanks to the partnership between Audi France and BP, when she took part in the French national series co-driven by Annie Arii. On the Terre de Garrigues and Causses Rouergats rallies she stormed to victories which, with all the marketing muscle of her employers at her back, became huge news.

Gaining speed and confidence with every outing, Mouton would make her first entry in the history books when she won the 1981 Sanremo Rally, beating all the boys by keeping out of trouble and attacking at precisely the right moment – a drive that she still relishes.

'For me, I remember two things: First, the mechanics were all there waiting for my co-driver Fabrizia Pons and me with a big bunch of flowers. Then they put the flowers on the car. That meant so much and was really important for us. Second, when you realised you won, there is nothing on top of that. I had this really fantastic feeling that we reached another level, maybe we will be able to win more.'

The 1982 season should have delivered the FIA World Rally Championship for Drivers but Mouton faced two great hurdles in that aim: Walter Röhrl's personal crusade against Audi and the absence of strategy that would define Audi's title-winning seasons in 1983 and 1984. As Hannu Mikkola said: they blew it.

In a recent interview, Roland Gumpert said: 'Michèle was as quick as the men, but she was fiery, and there'd always be more chance of her hitting a stone or something.' The statistics do

not bear this out, as from the start of the 1981 season to the start of her title charge, Mikkola and Mouton were level with two crashes each. Yes, she chose to park the car in Finland when she could have finished third, but there she was deliberately put on the least effective tyres.

From a distance of nearly 40 years, Mouton herself is unwilling to be too critical. 'Of course I have no memory of all of this,' she says. 'But if you are certain of what you are announcing, it would confirm the thesis that Audi did not believe much in the possibility of winning the championship with me and the final results dictated their decisions at the end.'

In 1983, Mouton dutifully followed team orders and shared, with Stig Blomqvist, in the job of guarding Mikkola's tail whenever possible. By that stage the stopwatches were showing that Blomqvist clearly had an edge over the rest of the Audi team and in 1984 Walter Röhrl was brought into the fold to spearhead the technical development.

For Mouton there was less to do but she seized upon the opportunity of taking the USA by storm at the Pikes Peak International Hill Climb. In 1982 and 1983, Audi USA's all-conquering champion John Buffum had rattled the cages of the good ol' boys when he entered his Quattro in 'the race to the clouds'. In 1984 there would be a full works effort with Michèle Mouton and the Audi Sport quattro.

ABOVE The sweetest moment came with victory on the 1981 Sanremo Rally. Mouton and Pons proved that they were not just a novelty attraction but genuine contenders. *(McKlein)*

Ivory Coast Rally. For 1986 she moved to Peugeot and crushed all opposition in the German national championship but, after the tragedies of the season and with the less exciting Group A cars on the horizon, she left the sport quite content with the honours that she had won.

Not that this was to be the end of Mouton's career. In tribute to her late friend Henri Toivonen, she established the Race of Champions as an annual jamboree for rally folk. Today it is a wildly profitable franchise embracing the cream of racing and rallying from around the world. Meanwhile, Mouton herself is back in the thick of the action as both manager of the FIA World Rally Championship and president of the FIA Women's Commission – spending her days wrestling with ways to make the sport better for all.

Stig Blomqvist

Born:
29 July 1946, Örebro, Sweden
World Rally Championship Victories:
11 (8 with Audi)
World Rally Championship Titles:
1984 (Audi)

With a father who was himself a keen amateur rally driver, Stig Blomqvist was able to indulge his passion for cars from a very young age – indeed, he co-drove for his father as early as the age of 12. By the time that he was old enough to hold a licence, Blomqvist was competing in rallies – and getting in the thick of the action with some seasoned campaigners.

Often working in cahoots with another aspiring star from Örebro, Per Eklund, the two young guns supplemented their incomes as driving instructors for the *Kvinnersta Folkhögskola* until both men were taken on by Saab as members of its works team.

Blomqvist got to master his craft as part of the tight-knit team from Trollhättan with its unique front-wheel-drive cars. He won the Swedish Rally for the first time in 1971 – the same year in which he also won his first RAC Rally. He would compete almost exclusively for Saab until 1981, when Saab gave up the unequal struggle to make its turbocharged car

The challenge of climbing 3km (2 miles) vertically on a 20km (12.5 mile) stretch of flat-out gravel sweepers enthralled her – although after solo practice runs she did ask for Fabrizia Pons to sit alongside and read the notes. With sheer drops measuring hundreds of metres in places, it was better to be safe than sorry. 'I felt the car really pushing me and you think, "Shit, I will go there!" I tell you, you are very close to... I had this feeling I was right there, so the feelings were very hot, I would say.'

In her first attempt she came second overall and was comfortably the fastest of the non-specialist roadsters built for the job. But that was not enough and so Mouton and Pons returned in 1985 with an adapted Sport quattro intent on winning the thing outright – which met with fierce resistance.

For a 5 mph breach of the recce speed rules, Mouton was ordered to push her car to the start line, get in and start it before she could go. 'The organisers made my life very complicated. It was like it was the first time they saw a rally car or a turbocharged car – even a European or a woman!' she would recall.

In the end she was allowed to start strapped in the car but was not allowed to select first gear until the flag fell. With her dander up, she duly rocketed up the hill to take the outright victory and set a new course record. It was to be the last hurrah of Mouton's time with Audi, which came to an end after the contentious

competitive and withdrew from the sport.

Eventually Blomqvist did a deal with Des O'Dell, the much-loved manager at Talbot, whose little Sunbeam Lotus was one of the most potent pre-Quattro rally cars. Adapting quickly to rear-wheel drive, Blomqvist's third place on the RAC Rally secured Talbot the manufacturers' world championship. Almost immediately, Peugeot took control of the rally programme, with former co-driver Jean Todt being given the reins. He wanted a star to develop and drive his new Group B car, the Peugeot 205 T16, but before he knew it Blomqvist was gone – to Audi.

'Ah it was fantastic really,' Blomqvist recalled. 'I remember the first time I went down to Ingolstadt and got to drive in the car and I couldn't believe the difference between two-wheel drive and four-wheel drive because that's like day and night.'

Also like day and night was the way in which Blomqvist drove the Audi Quattro. Team leader Hannu Mikkola's driving style was smooth and fluid, and he had never needed to adapt the left-foot braking technique that front-wheel-drive cars demand. Blomqvist immediately felt at home in the understeering Audi and used his left foot to provoke incredible behaviour in the corners, throwing the car's tail to corner in a perfect arc.

'It was a big step from everything else, so that was an evolution for the rally I think and everybody had to gear up a bit and get something sorted,' Blomqvist remembered. 'Yeah, okay, they are nice looking and the sound is nice, the speed between the corners is quite good and they're quite exciting I think.'

Blomqvist was engaged by Audi's Swedish importer to contest the national rally championship in 1982 – and he won every round. Audi Sport also called upon his services in Sweden's round of the World Rally Championship and, again, Blomqvist won. In the autumn, Audi Sport needed a reliable pair of hands to score points to prise Opel's grasp from

the manufacturers' title and to support Michèle Mouton's bid for the drivers' title. In the end he scored 35 points on the 1,000 Lakes and Sanremo rallies, compared with Mouton's 10.

The idea of being a team player in the sense of handing over a hard-won position was something of an anathema to the Swede. So too was talking about the job to the media. In the car is simply where he has always been happiest, and out of it he has the ability to make modern-day Formula 1 'Iceman' Kimi Räikkönen look as needy and attention-seeking as a reality TV starlet.

The European press of the day loved to give drivers nicknames – although Blomqvist clearly perplexed them. Where Hannu Mikkola was 'the flying Finn' and Michèle Mouton was 'the devil with the face of an angel' then Blomqvist was 'the lonely man of the forests'.

The Swede played second fiddle to Mikkola's charge for the drivers' championship in 1983 and also took over the Finn's seat in Audi UK's car in the British championship – which he won. But the payback for these labours came in 1984, when Blomqvist became *de facto* team leader and the rest of the Audi team was there to support him.

'The team was really strong and they knew what to do so it was a very, very good time and we were very hard to beat – and winning the

championship was a nice feeling,' he chuckled. 'When I was winning the championship I think we stayed about 290 days at hotels. We were never at home, actually.'

In 1985, Audi plummeted in terms of competitiveness, and Blomqvist intensely disliked the short wheelbase cars. His ideal Audi would have married the Quattro A2 with the 550 bhp engine from the Sport quattro S1 – but having committed so much resource to the short cars, a hybrid was never going to happen. In the end, Blomqvist left Audi at the end of 1985 and did a deal with Ford.

He remained with Ford until the 1990s, when the rise of front-wheel-drive classes in national series and the F2 World Championship saw Blomqvist's skills high in demand – most notably with Škoda, where this author had the bittersweet job of doing his public relations work.

The downside to the job was presenting him for interviews – occasions that he generally loathed. The upsides included his staggering third place overall on the snowy 1996 RAC Rally in a tiny 1,600cc Škoda – beaten only by two works WRC cars and in front of much four-wheel-drive turbo technology – and catching a ride on a media event to witness him in full flight. In the midst of the ditch-hopping pandemonium there was a look of absolute serenity to Stig, just the lightest fingertip control

BELOW Stig in his happy place: now as then, the best environment in which to spend time with Blomqvist is when he has a wheel in his hands and ideally some snow underfoot. *(Audi AG)*

on the wheel as his feet danced away below decks to summon up the speed, the direction and the attitude at which he wished to be travelling. It was a five-minute masterclass.

The lonely man of the forests? Not at all. On the morning after the 1996 RAC, most of the team crawled out of bed with thick heads and checked out of the hotel, only to find Stig sat regally in the bar, surrounded by adoring rally men. His front-line career lasted until 2006, since when he has been a regular front runner in historic competition and attended many an Audi reunion, while also proudly watching his son Tom's career in Deutsche Tourenwagen Masters (DTM) touring cars.

Walter Röhrl

Born:
  7 March 1947, Regensburg, Germany
World Rally Championship Victories:
  14 (2 with Audi)
World Rally Championship Titles:
  1980, 1982

The three Röhrl children grew up with their mother, and in time youngest son Walter found himself drawn towards the Church. He worked as a legal representative of the Bishop of Regensburg across the seven diocese of Bavaria – a job that often required him to drive quite rapidly between engagements.

Oldest brother Michael had bought an old Porsche 356 and encouraged his young brother's keen interest in cars and driving. Sadly, Michael Röhrl died in a road accident, a devastating blow to the younger brother who idolised him, but soon a work colleague called Herbert Marecek pointed Walter towards rally driving, acting as sponsor and co-driver.

By 1970, Röhrl's talents were becoming evident and he was offered a paid drive with Ford – albeit while still working for the Church. After his first season with the team, the youngster bowed to pressure from his mother and announced his retirement, but then thought better of it. In 1972 he really made his name by beating established stars like Hannu Mikkola and Jean-Pierre Nicolas on the 1972 Olympic Rally, at the wheel of an unfancied Ford Capri.

For 1973, Opel offered Röhrl a full-time

drive and he bade farewell to the diocese, going on to finish second in the European Rally Championship in his first season and winning it in 1974. Yet throughout his career, the Church was never far away, no matter how far or how fast he drove. 'I am very faithful,' he later said.

'I prayed a lot under the worst competitive pressure. Sometimes I feel guilty nowadays because I pray less. Because back then, when I needed help, I prayed more. It's kind of shabby, I think. I used to have a language rule at the rallies: "You do not have to help me win. Just help me, that nothing happens to me." So I prayed, when I stood on the [start line]. To demand a victory would have seemed rude to me.'

Combining racing with rallying in the mid-1970s took some direction out of Röhrl's career until he was approached by former Lancia and Ferrari team boss Daniele Audetto to join his new squad at Fiat. Audetto teamed Röhrl with a laid-back and gregarious co-driver, Christian Geistdörfer, and the results culminated in them romping off with the 1980 World Rally Championship title.

So great was his satisfaction at winning the 1980 Monte Carlo Rally that Röhrl almost announced his retirement on the spot – then the novelty of a championship title beckoned so he stayed on. Fiat then withdrew at the end of

ABOVE Röhrl's talent put him at the top table, both in rallying and circuit racing, sharing a car with Formula 1 icon Gilles Villeneuve in his years at Fiat. *(McKlein)*

the year, which left two German manufacturers vying for the Bavarian's services in 1981: Mercedes-Benz and Audi.

Röhrl visited Ingolstadt twice, each time taking one of the prototype Quattros out for a test drive, exactly as Hannu Mikkola had done. As a local boy, the whole situation seemed perfect, yet after his second visit Röhrl went straight to Stuttgart. 'All of the technical people, or leading technical people in Mercedes said "this thing will never work so don't worry about that. We are doing the right thing and forget about Audi,"' Christian Geistdörfer recalled.

AMG, the competition arm of Mercedes-Benz, was planning a five-year campaign. Röhrl was promised a powerful 5-litre 500 SLC as his Group 4 car in 1981–82, after which Mercedes would build a lightweight four-wheel-drive car to Group B regulations. In the end, Röhrl chose to make his bed in Stuttgart.

Audi team principal Walter Treser was furious and vented his frustration in the German media. Röhrl meanwhile discovered that the board at Mercedes-Benz was less enthusiastic about the programme than might have been believed, after he suffered a testing crash when preparing for the Monte Carlo Rally. A delivery truck had been permitted to enter the section of closed roads he was using, resulting in a sizeable scandal.

In the fallout from that accident, one of the Mercedes board members telephoned Röhrl directly and asked if he was going to win the Monte Carlo Rally. The ever-truthful driver stated that if it snowed they might get lucky and finish

in the top five, but without snow he couldn't guarantee where they would be in the top 15. Facing the ignominy of being shown the way by a motley assortment of Fords, Renaults and Talbots, Mercedes cancelled its five-year programme almost overnight.

'I already had a bad feeling about the Mercedes deal,' Röhrl reflected. 'I felt I was like everyone else, only looking for the money. So when the board decided to withdraw, it was like a relief for my conscience. And then I had a telephone call from Porsche, who said they had no money but asked if I would like to drive their car. It was the start of a big friendship.'

Röhrl had fun in 1981, but he had a job to do: beating Audi. To this end a marriage of inconvenience was agreed with Opel, the only team capable of giving him a works car for 1982. Team principal Tony Fall had landed a major sponsor for his team – the cigarette brand Rothmans – and spent a good deal of that money on getting the Bavarian into his cars. Fall was therefore less than amused to discover that his star driver was a committed non-smoker who refused to do any promotional work for Rothmans.

'I did not speak for three minutes in eleven months with Tony Fall,' Röhrl later said. 'It did not exist for me.'

The only thing that did exist to him was a conviction to exact revenge for the humiliating furore that had taken place a year earlier. 'When I signed for Mercedes at the end of 1980 I also had an offer from Audi and their manager, Walter Treser, was very angry that I did not accept it,' Röhrl said.

'He did lots of interviews with bad comments about me so when I went back to the world championship in 1982 my principal motivation was to beat the Audis and stop them being world champion. For them to be beaten by me in an Opel with old technology was awful.'

The 1982 season was a true nail-biter as Opel's cantankerous star went head-to-head with the darling of the World Rally Championship, Michèle Mouton. With the drivers' title settled in his favour, Röhrl rather grudgingly set off for the RAC Rally to help Opel claim the manufacturers' prize. Before the rally started, however, it was announced that he would join Lancia for 1983 and Tony Fall decided that enough was enough – he sent his new champion home with another very public rebuke. To this day he cares little for Opel and never even collected his champion's trophy.

Röhrl's season with Lancia did not bring a third world championship – mainly because he didn't want one. Titles did not interest him, only being the fastest rally driver on the greatest rallies in the world, and Lancia team principal Cesare Fiorio was happy to indulge him if it helped win the manufacturers' prize. Thanks to Röhrl's inspired victories in Monte Carlo and the Acropolis, Audi was denied the title that it so dearly craved – and then finally an olive branch was extended from the very top in Ingolstadt.

'Audi board member Dr Sonnenborn was a critical influence in making me switch to Audi,' Röhrl said. 'As I understood it, he had been given an order by Piëch: "Bring in Röhrl. Driving with him is much cheaper than driving against him."'

With Lancia, Röhrl had listed a handful of rallies in which he was interested in driving. With Audi, he nailed it down to just one rally and for one reason: Stig Blomqvist.

'Stig was the only one I'd never competed against in the same car. All the rest – Mikkola, Waldegård, Alén, Vatanen – I had been in the same car at the same time. I wanted to know, because everyone said Stig was the fastest man with four-wheel drive, the fastest on snow. It was a big motivation for me. I said to Audi, I will help you and one of your pilots to be world champion. But in Monte Carlo I want to show who is chief!'

It seemed remarkable to his teammates that a man who had been forced to dig so deep in order to prevent them from winning championships was now quite content not to pick the lower-hanging fruit for himself. 'He was very good and very quick and very, very professional because he knew what he was doing and he really tried everything and he was… okay… he was a bit different,' reflected Blomqvist.

Where Röhrl's interest lay at Audi was in the development of better Quattros. Both the Audi Sport quattro and the Audi Sport quattro S1 were the focal point of his time: trying to make these skittish, wildly over-powered cars into contenders against the perfectly weighted new

generation of Group B thoroughbreds like the Peugeot 205 T16.

Working in isolation from the rest of the rally world, Röhrl was content communing with the laws of traction and polar inertia… it came much easier to him than the frat-house antics of his fellow drivers.

'If we had a special stage and there was a delay, everybody would get out of the cars and talk together,' he reflected. 'I would sit in the car, Christian would be reading his notes, and I never talked to anyone… They were thinking I didn't like them, but it was just my opinion of how to be professional. Nothing else… It was funny because I liked all of them, I had no problems with anybody.'

Walter Röhrl's mesmerising victory by six-and-a-half minutes in the 1985 Sanremo Rally was to be the last for an Audi Quattro in the world championship – and it was all down to his obstinate determination to turn the gargantuan power and colossal investment into a winner.

He would do it all again two years later in the epic Pikes Peak International Hill Climb (see Chapter 4), in another highly personal battle with Peugeot. Then he turned his back on rallying and joined Audi's squad in circuit racing in Trans-Am, IMSA and the DTM before re-joining Porsche to take part at Le Mans and to develop its road cars, finally retiring at the age of 70.

In 2019, Röhrl became the first rally driver to be inducted into the FIA's Hall of Fame – it is an accolade that this singularly brilliant man richly deserved.

ABOVE Very few people saw the gentle giant that Röhrl allows himself to be today. In competition, and in his exhaustive testing duties, he was the epitome of single-minded professionalism. *(McKlein)*

Chapter Four

Anatomy of the Audi Quattro

Audi's design team took a lot of good ideas that people had produced in the past and brought them all together with a flourish, thereby creating the Quattro. Turning a road car into a competition vehicle meant testing its reliability to extremes, leading to the development of new and better parts to bring strength, lose weight and gain higher and higher speeds against staggering opposition.

OPPOSITE Roland Gumpert oversees the servicing of the Audi Quattro in 1981. *(McKlein)*

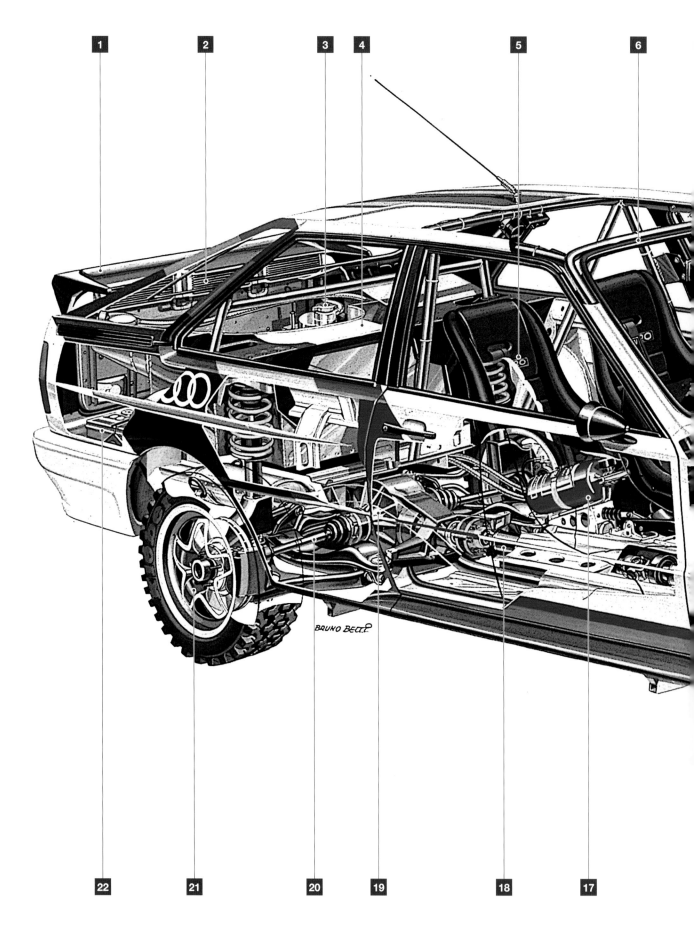

BRUNO BETTI

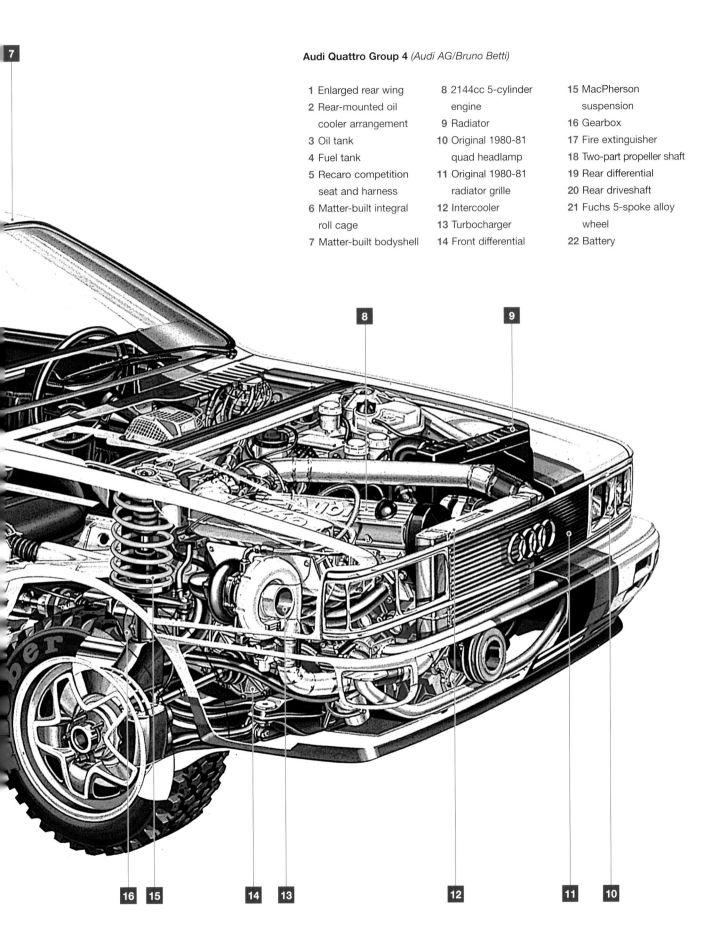

Audi Quattro Group 4 (*Audi AG/Bruno Betti*)

1 Enlarged rear wing
2 Rear-mounted oil cooler arrangement
3 Oil tank
4 Fuel tank
5 Recaro competition seat and harness
6 Matter-built integral roll cage
7 Matter-built bodyshell

8 2144cc 5-cylinder engine
9 Radiator
10 Original 1980-81 quad headlamp
11 Original 1980-81 radiator grille
12 Intercooler
13 Turbocharger
14 Front differential

15 MacPherson suspension
16 Gearbox
17 Fire extinguisher
18 Two-part propeller shaft
19 Rear differential
20 Rear driveshaft
21 Fuchs 5-spoke alloy wheel
22 Battery

Specifications

	Audi Quattro Group 4	Audi Quattro A1
Years active	1980–82	1983–86
Class	Group 4/Group B	Group B
Floorpan	Volkswagen B2	Volkswagen B2
Construction	Steel unitary body Typ 85 with integrated roll cage, internal chassis rails and front/rear subframe	Steel unitary body Typ 85 with integrated roll cage, Kevlar and carbon fibre panels, internal chas rails and front/rear subframe
Homologation date	01/01/1980	01/01/1983
Homologation no.	671	B229
Engine layout	Longitudinal ahead of front axle, mounted 27.5 degrees from vertical	Longitudinal ahead of front axle, mounted 27.5 degrees from verti
Number of cylinders	5, single belt-driven overhead camshaft	5, single belt-driven overhead camshaft
Engine construction	Iron block	Aluminium block with GG cast iro cylinder liners
Cylinder head	Reverse flow cast aluminium alloy with hemispherical combustion chambers and vertical valves	Reverse flow cast aluminium allo with hemispherical combustion chambers and vertical valves
Number of valves	10 (inlet 38.2mm/outlet 33.3mm)	10 (inlet 41.1mm/outlet 35.2mm)
Bore x stroke	79.5 x 86.4	79.5 x 86.4
Cubic capacity	2,144 cc	2,144 cc
FIA capacity (x 1.4)	3,003 cc	3,003 cc
Compression ratio	6:3:1	6:3:1
Ignition	Bosch	Bosch
Firing order	1-2-4-5-3	1-2-4-5-3
Max. power/rpm	340bhp / 5,500rpm	360bhp / 6,500rpm
Max. torque/rpm	412Nm / 3,500rpm	412Nm / 3,500rpm
Fuel injection	Pierburg	Pierburg
Engine management	Hitachi	Hitachi
Turbocharger	KKK K26 with intercooler	KKK K26 with intercooler
Turbo pressure	1.5–1.8 bar	0.8–1.9 bar
Wastegate	Audi	Audi
Cooling system	Jacketed water-cooled with pump, radiator, fan and thermostat	Jacketed water-cooled with pum radiator, fan and thermostat
Lubrication system	Dry sump with rear-mounted 12-litre tank and external oil cooler	Dry sump with rear-mounted 12-litre tank and external oil cool
Transmission	Permanent 4WD	Permanent 4WD with centre differential
Front/rear split	50/50	50/50

udi Quattro A2	Audi Sport quattro	Audi Sport quattro S1	Audi Sport quattro S1 Pikes Peak
983–86	1984–87	1985–88	1987
roup B	Group B	Group B	Open Rally
olkswagen B2	Bespoke	Bespoke	Bespoke
teel unitary body Typ 85 with ntegrated titanium roll cage, evlar and carbon fibre panels, nternal chassis rails and front/ ear subframe	Steel unitary body with integrated titanium roll cage, Kevlar and carbon fibre panels, internal chassis rails and front/ rear subframe	Steel unitary body with integrated titanium roll cage, Kevlar and carbon fibre panels, internal chassis rails and front/ rear subframe	Spaceframe with integrated titanium roll cage, Kevlar and carbon fibre body, internal chassis rails and front/rear subframe
1/07/1983	01/05/1984	01/07/1985	N/A
243	B264	B264	N/A
ongitudinal ahead of front axle, ounted 27.5 degrees from ertical	Longitudinal ahead of front axle, mounted 27.5 degrees from vertical	Longitudinal ahead of front axle	Longitudinal ahead of front axle
single belt-driven overhead amshaft	5, twin belt-driven overhead camshafts	5, twin belt-driven overhead camshafts	5, twin belt-driven overhead camshafts
luminium block with GG cast on cylinder liners	Aluminium block with GG cast iron cylinder liners	Aluminium block with GG cast iron cylinder liners	Aluminium block with GG cast iron cylinder liners
everse flow cast aluminium loy with hemispherical ombustion chambers and ertical valves	Cross flow cast aluminium alloy with hemispherical combustion chambers	Cross flow cast aluminium alloy with hemispherical combustion chambers	Cross flow cast aluminium alloy with hemispherical combustion chambers
0 (inlet 41.1mm/outlet 35.2mm)	20 (inlet 32.2mm/outlet 28.2mm)	20 (inlet 32.2mm/outlet 28.2mm)	20 (inlet 32.2mm/outlet 28.2mm)
5.5 x 86.4	79.5 x 85	79.5 x 85	79.5 x 85
110, 2,121 or 2,135 cc	2,110 cc	2,121 cc	2,121 cc
954, 2,969 or 2,989 cc	2,954 cc	2,969 cc	N/A
5:1	7:5:1	7:5:1	8:6:1
osch	Bosch electronic	Bosch electronic	Bosch electronic
2-4-5-3	1-2-4-5-3	1-2-4-5-3	1-2-4-5-3
bhp / 6,500rpm	510bhp / 7,500rpm	550bhp / 7,500rpm	750bhp / 8,000rpm
0Nm / 3,400rpm	460Nm / 4,500rpm	550Nm / 5,500rpm	590Nm / 5,500rpm
erburg/Bosch	Bosch	Bosch	Bosch
tachi/Bosch	Bosch	Bosch	Bosch
KK K27 with intercooler	KKK K27 with intercooler	KKK K28 with intercooler	KKK K28 with intercooler
8–1.9 bar	1.7–2.0 bar	1.9–2.2 bar	3.0 bar
di	Porsche-derived 'Umluft'	Porsche-derived 'Umluft'	Porsche-derived 'Umluft'
acketed water-cooled with mp, radiator, fan and ermostat	Jacketed water-cooled with pump, radiator, fan and thermostat	Jacketed water-cooled with rear-mounted pump, radiator, fan and thermostat	Jacketed water-cooled with rear-mounted pump, radiator, fan and thermostat
y sump with rear-mounted tch tank and external oil oler	Dry sump with rear-mounted catch tank and external oil cooler	Dry sump with rear-mounted 12-litre tank and oil cooler	Dry sump with rear-mounted catch tank and oil cooler
ermanent 4WD with centre ferential	Permanent 4WD with centre differential	Permanent 4WD with Torsen Gleason or Ferguson centre differential	Permanent 4WD with Torsen Gleason centre differential
/50	50/50	Variable	Variable

	Audi Quattro Group 4	Audi Quattro A1
Gearbox	5-speed manual	5-speed manual
Clutch	Fichtel & Sachs dry single-plate 240mm	Fichtel & Sachs dry single-plate 240mm
Suspension	MacPherson with front and rear anti-roll bar	MacPherson with front and rear anti-roll bar
Dampers	Boge coil spring, telescopic gas shock	Boge coil spring, telescopic gas shock
Brakes	Dual circuit with vacuum servo, standard ratio split front to rear: 60–40%	Dual circuit with vacuum servo, standard ratio split front to rear: 60–40%
Brake discs	**Gravel/snow**: AP front ventilated discs 280mm diameter with 1 piston calliper 54mm diameter, rear solid discs 245mm diameter with 1 piston calliper 36mm diameter. **Asphalt**: AP four piston calipers 42.5mm diameter	**Gravel/snow:** AP front ventilated discs 280mm diameter with 1 cast iron piston calliper 54mm diameter, rear solid discs 245mm diameter with 1 cast iron piston calliper 36mm diameter. **Asphalt:** AP front 280/295/305mm diameter with four aluminium piston calipers 42.5mm diameter, rear 280/295/305mm diameter with four aluminium piston calipers 42.5mm diameter
Steering	Rack and pinion with hydraulic servo assistance	Rack and pinion with hydraulic servo assistance
Wheels	6j x 16 (snow) 7j x 16 (gravel) 10j x 16 (asphalt)	6j x 16 (snow) 7-9j x 16 (gravel) 10j x 16 (asphalt)
Tyres	Kleber Timi (snow tyres) Pirelli (UK, Italy) Michelin (Sweden)	Kleber Timi (snow tyres) Pirelli (UK, Italy) Michelin (Sweden)
Length	4,404mm	4,404mm
Width	1,733mm	1,837mm
Wheelbase	2,524mm	2,524mm
Track	Front: 1,465mm Rear: 1,502mm	Front: 1,465mm Rear: 1,502mm
Weight	1,150kg	1,120kg
Weight distribution	60/40	60/40
Fuel capacity	90–120 litres	90–200 litres
WRC starts/finishes (average)	82/40 (48.8%)	25/14 (58.3%)
WRC points scored	194	84

Audi Quattro A2	Audi Sport quattro	Audi Sport quattro S1	Audi Sport quattro S1 Pikes Peak
/6-speed manual	6-speed manual	6-speed manual/Porsche PDK semi-auto	6-speed manual
Fichtel & Sachs dry single-plate 240mm	Fichtel & Sachs dry single-plate 240mm	Fichtel & Sachs or Porsche/AP twin plate	Fichtel & Sachs twin plate
MacPherson with front and rear radius arms and anti-roll bar	MacPherson with front and rear radius arms and anti-roll bar (19–28mm diameter)	MacPherson with front and rear radius arms and anti-roll bar (19–28mm diameter)	MacPherson with front and rear radius arms and anti-roll bar (19–28mm diameter)
Boge coil spring, telescopic gas shock	Boge coil spring, telescopic gas shock	Boge coil spring, telescopic gas shock	Boge coil spring, telescopic gas shock
Dual circuit with vacuum servo, standard ratio split front to rear: 60–40%	Dual circuit with vacuum servo, variable ratio split front to rear	Dual circuit with vacuum servo, variable ratio split front to rear	Dual circuit with vacuum servo, variable ratio split front to rear
Gravel/snow: AP front ventilated discs 280mm diameter with 1 cast iron piston calliper 54mm diameter, rear solid discs 245mm diameter with 1 cast iron piston calliper 36mm diameter. **Asphalt:** AP front 280/295/305mm diameter with four aluminium piston calipers 42.5mm diameter, rear 280/295/305mm diameter with four aluminium piston calipers 42.5mm	**Gravel/snow:** Lockheed or Girling front ventilated discs 295mm diameter with 4 aluminium piston calipers 41.3mm diameter, rear ventilated discs 295mm diameter with 4 aluminium piston calipers 41.3mm diameter. **Asphalt:** Lockheed or Girling ventilated discs all around 280/304/330mm diameter with 4 aluminium piston calipers 42.5/43mm diameter. **1985:** front ventilated discs with water cooling 330mm diameter with 2 x 2-piston calipers 2x44.4 + 2x40.7mm diameter, rear ventilated discs 280mm diameter with 4 aluminium piston calipers 31/33.9/34.9mm diameter.	**Gravel/snow:** Lockheed or Girling front ventilated discs 295mm diameter with 4 aluminium piston calipers 41.3mm diameter, rear ventilated discs 295mm diameter with 4 aluminium piston calipers 41.3mm diameter. **Asphalt:** front ventilated discs with water cooling 330mm diameter with 2 x 2-piston calipers 2x44.4 + 2x40.7mm diameter, rear ventilated discs 280mm diameter with 4 aluminium piston calipers 31/33.9/34.9mm diameter.	Lockheed or Girling front ventilated discs 295mm diameter with 4 aluminium piston calipers 41.3mm diameter, rear ventilated discs 295mm diameter with 4 aluminium piston calipers 41.3mm diameter.
Rack and pinion with hydraulic servo assistance	Rack and pinion with hydraulic servo assistance	Rack and pinion with hydraulic servo assistance	Rack and pinion with hydraulic servo assistance
x 16 (snow) -9j x 16 (gravel) Oj x 16 (asphalt) 1j x 15 (asphalt)	6j x 16 (snow) 7j-8j x 16 (gravel) 9j-10j x 16 (asphalt) 10j x 15 (asphalt)	6j x 16 (snow) 7j-8j x 16 (gravel) 9j- x 16 (asphalt)	8j x 16
Michelin Pirelli (UK)	Michelin Pirelli (UK)	Michelin Pirelli (Ulster Rally)	Michelin
404mm	4,160mm	4,240mm	4,240mm
837mm	1,817mm	1,860mm	1,860mm
524mm	2,204mm	2,224mm	2,224mm
Front: 1,465mm Rear: 1,502mm	Front: 1,490mm Rear: 1,520mm	Front: 1,490mm Rear: 1,520mm	Front: 1,490mm Rear: 1,520mm
000kg	1,220kg	1,100kg	950kg
0/40	63/37	58/52	50/50
0–200 litres	30–200 litres	30–120 litres	30 litres
3/52 (55.9%)	27/12 (44%)	9/4 (44.4%)	N/A
51	96	34	N/A

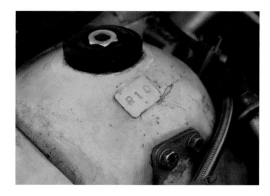

Bodywork, chassis and aerodynamics

The bodyshell of every Audi Quattro for competition use was built by the specialists at Matter , who went through the production line article with a fine-toothed comb and hand-crafted each example with the lessons learnt from previous testing and competition experience.

Effectively, every car from Matter was a hand-built original, including the fully integrated roll cage, and each new shell was given a stamp bearing its production number; R1 being the first prototype rally car. By the end of 1983 more than 50 cars had been built and the numbers kept rising in the development of the heavily modified Audi Sport quattro in both standard and aerodynamically enhanced S1 configurations.

With the Group 4 cars, the major preoccupation initially was in reducing the Quattro's hefty bulk. A regular rear-wheel drive

Group 4 car like a Ford Escort RS1800 would tip the scales at little more than 900kg (1,984lb), whereas on its debut at the 1981 Monte Carlo Rally the fully laden Quattros weighed 1,240kg (2,734lb).

Almost immediately, the job of the historian (not to mention that of subsequent owners and vendors seeking provenance) became rather complicated. For example, in Portugal 1981, the third event of the Quattro's rally career, the results of Matter's use of thinner gauge steel gave a stated weight of 1,040kg (2,293lb) for Michèle Mouton's newly built gravel car, compared to 1,080kg (2,381lb) for Hannu Mikkola's example.

Yet the registration plate on Mouton's car was IN-NV 90, which had been carried by Mikkola on his victorious solo outing in Sweden three weeks earlier – the same car that won the Jänner Rallye as the Quattro's first victory (using a different engine). It would not be the last time that such a phenomenon occurred.

From early in the programme, Matter and Audi Sport were able to tailor the build of each shell to the demands of the event that it was to compete in – just the same as any other component like the tyres. At one end of the scale were cars intended for the Tour de Corse, which must be as light as possible for turning in to and powering out of the hairpins. A standard shell would suit Monte Carlo or Sanremo and then the weight would go upwards depending on how much reinforcement was needed.

The most durable and heavyweight cars

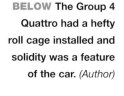

ABOVE LEFT Quattro IN-NV 90, in which Franz Wittmann won the 1981 Jänner Rally, was fitted with a new engine and won the Swedish Rally in Hannu Mikkola's hands. *(McKlein)*

ABOVE IN-NV 90 then reappeared in Portugal, painted black – and fitted with a new lightweight shell. *(McKlein)*

were destined for Africa, for which numerous reinforcements and mounting points were needed – together with an enlarged fuel tank capable of holding 200 litres to cover the long stages. On the lightweight cars, one of the earliest modifications externally was the fitting of 'eyebrow' wheel arch extensions to allow the fitting of wider racing tyres of up to 10 inches across for asphalt rallying.

One aspect that all of the competition Quattros shared was the relocation of the battery from the nose to the boot, for obvious weight distribution reasons. The downside of this was that the battery was surrounded by the neck and body of the fuel tank which, in the group B era particularly, was prone to springing a leak if the toluene-heavy brews of the day compromised the integrity of a rubber seal. The drivers chose not to think about carrying a potential bomb around in the boot, however.

Mitigating this, at least in part, was that Matter built box-like chassis rails into each of its shells, through which the fuel and hydraulic lines would be run. This helped to insulate them to the greater extent and ensure that no amount of rocks or other obstacles could cause breakage and potential disaster.

By the time of the Audi Quattro A2, the difference between a lightweight shell and a beefier example to cope with the 1,000

BELOW LEFT The first body modification was adding 'eyebrow' extensions to the maximum permitted body width, allowing for the widest asphalt tyres possible. *(Author)*

BELOW The beautifully crafted fuel tank fills most of the boot space, with the spare wheel, oil tank and battery. *(Author)*

Lakes was more than 200kg (441lb). The real heavyweights in Audi Sport's arsenal were the cars intended for Africa.

When the team prepared for the 1982 Ivory Coast Rally, Matter reinforced the welds and buttressed the joints in 50 places around the car, put in additional vibration damping and cooling ducts as well as fitting 'roo bars and additional spotlights on the scuttle panel. From this specification, future Safari and Ivory Coast entries would progressively get lighter until they were broadly similar to an Acropolis specification.

The early aerodynamics of the Quattro were lifted wholesale from the road cars. At the sharp end, the standard quad headlamp arrangement was retained on either side of the standard radiator grille, all of which fine detail was somewhat obscured by the mountings for the Carello spotlights, which could carry one, two or three extra lamps, depending upon requirements. At the 1981 Acropolis Rally, Walter Treser elected to remove the inner headlights from the arrangement and fit a flap in the space that would open to allow cool air in – and his team was promptly excluded as a result.

Incoming technical chief Roland Gumpert then oversaw the hurried replacement drawn up and passed by the FIA and this was the definitive 'face' of the Audi Quattro that it would wear until the advent of the Audi Sport quattro. The radiator grille was broader and trapezoid in shape, giving the car a pronounced overbite, and on the Group B cars was formed from composite material. Just one of the standard headlights remained on either side of the new structure – and Audi's cooling worries were thus becalmed.

At the rear of the car, Audi Sport started out with a mildly enlarged boot lid spoiler when compared with the road cars. The

RIGHT The first iteration of the Audi Quattro grille was barely different from that of the road car until the Acropolis Rally headlight debacle. *(Author)*

RIGHT The team responded quickly to homologate a competition radiator grille to make cooling more effective. *(Author)*

LEFT The oil cooler was removed from behind the front grille and placed beneath an enlarged rear spoiler. The space up front was filled by a larger intercooler.

seventh appearance of the Quattros in world championship trim, the 1981 Sanremo Rallye, saw Audi Sport arrive with a very different structure in place, the result of extensive work by Gumpert and homologation engineer Jürgen Bertl to kill several birds with one stone.

The enlarged wing effectively created a frame inside which the oil cooler was housed, allowing a free flow of air at all times to help stem the tide of engine-related retirements. In addition to enhanced cooling, moving the oil cooler outdoors also removed a weighty item from the nose of the car and helped in its modest way in addressing the main problem of the Quattro's design – its nose-heavy weight distribution.

Ferdinand Piëch's five-cylinder engine was a lusty gem but its installation was troublesome. It sat longitudinally in front of the front axle in a crowded engine bay, giving the Quattro a 60/40 weight distribution, which dulled its turn-in and provoked occasionally epic understeer behaviour. Pulling weight rearwards was a huge preoccupation throughout the Quattro's competition life, and although the absence of the oil coolers helped, the space that it left was soon filled by enlarged turbos and intercoolers.

For 1983, Audi Sport had to produce its cars to Group B specification, and this presented Matter with a whole raft of changes to consider. Firstly, the construction of the cars was virtually free, allowing for the introduction of exotic, lightweight composites in fabricating the body panels. As early as the 1982 Swedish Rally, the boot lid was made from Kevlar. Soon this would become the primary material used in the body.

The interim Audi Quattro A1 had new Kevlar wings hung on each corner, filling the maximum permitted body width and able to house the widest possible asphalt tyres without the need for eyebrow extensions. A vent cut into the rear arches assisted in cooling the rear brakes, with more vents appearing in the nose of the car, on which the bonnet was made from what was then termed 'space-age carbon fibre'.

Reducing the sheet metal to a minimum at the front required Matter to completely redesign the front impact structure. A robust spaceframe was created that was then dressed in the composite panels, into which the engine and transmission would later be fitted. When fully prepared for a rally, the quoted weight given for the A1 was 1,130kg (2,491lb), which may sound like an anathema when the Quattro was 1,080 but the A1 was classed as an 'over 3-litre' car once its turbo was taken into account, which meant a minimum weight of 1,100kg (2,425lb). All that would change with the arrival of the next car.

Within four months, the Audi Quattro A1 was superseded in front-line service by the Audi Quattro A2. The A2 had a fractionally smaller engine and thus dropped into the lower capacity class of 'up to 3 litres' with a reduced minimum weight of 960kg (2,116lb). On their debut at the 1983 Tour de Corse, using titanium for the roll cage, the Quattro A2s were quoted as weighing 'just under 1,000 kilograms'.

The easiest way to tell the A2 apart from the A1 was that the later car had a more pronounced flare to its rear wheel arches, beginning much further forward along the sill and giving a much more muscular look to its haunches. Not only that, but the A2 had a second vent cut in above the first, through which air was channelled to cool the rear differential.

ABOVE A sturdy structure lies beneath the shapely Kevlar – Audi drivers always felt confident that they were in a robust car. *(Author)*

RIGHT Standard doors were gutted and re-skinned with Kevlar on the earlier Group B cars. *(Author)*

ABOVE Functional ducting to cool the rear brakes and differential are the only break in a seamless panel fit. *(Author)*

Many revisions would be made to the A1 and A2 in the course of a competition career that lasted right up to the end of Group B rallying, both in the hands of the works team and its private customers. Among these was a slight rise in the floorpan from front to rear of the cars built after the start of 1984, intended to coax weight distribution backwards along the longitudinal axis and resulting in what Hannu Mikkola and Stig Blomqvist agreed were the best-handling Quattros of all.

There was to be no such fiddling with the details for the next step in the Quattro's evolution, however. In September 1983, Audi showed off a new concept car at the Frankfurt Motor Show that it called the Audi Sport quattro. This rather dramatic-looking vehicle was a Matter-crafted road car upon which

BELOW The final step was to fabricate a bespoke competition door entirely from lightweight materials – with a string acting as the handle. *(Author)*

ABOVE The Group 4 cars retained standard construction and details, simply adapted for competition use. *(Author)*

RIGHT The Group B doors were effectively bare frames clad in Kevlar. *(Author)*

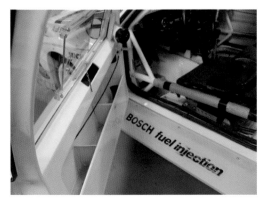

the most obvious change was a dramatic shortening of the wheelbase from 2,524mm on the standard road cars, Group 4 and Group B cars to just 2,204mm on the new model.

Radical surgery had been needed – the cut coming from between the B-pillar and rear wheel arch – to produce a rather caricatured quattro, from which the capital 'Q' had also been shorn. Most observers were so flabbergasted by this dwarfish creation, not to mention the fact that it had four valves per cylinder, that they failed to notice that the windscreen was mounted at a considerably steeper angle.

The rationale behind the car came entirely from the rally team. As early as 1981, the Audi Sport engineers had been investigating ways in which to make their cars more competitive on asphalt, particularly the tortuous roads of Corsica upon which they were always at a disadvantage. While they were discussing all of the various modifications, Hannu Mikkola chimed in to suggest that the original Quattro's rakish windscreen was very stylish but did cause some issues with visibility due to reflecting the sunlight badly.

The simplest solution was therefore to take the more upright windscreen and A-pillars, together with the scuttle, firewall and other accoutrements, from the standard Audi 80 saloon and graft them on to the truncated quattro pan. The public response to the 'concept car' in Frankfurt was overwhelmingly positive, and as a result Audi signed off on a limited production run of 200 cars, each to be hand-built by Mätter and Audi Sport, that would go on sale direct from the factory at the staggering price of DM200,000 (or £50,000/$75,000 in 1983), which was double that of the standard Quattro.

Of course, 200 units was the requirement for homologating the new car for competition, and thus the Audi Sport quattro became the preferred choice of the rally team management from the 1984 Tour de Corse onwards. The problem was that, as far as the majority of their drivers were concerned, they were much better off with the old cars.

Shortening the wheelbase of the Quattro had the rather unfortunate side-effect of undoing all the good work on weight distribution. When it went into competition, a thumping 63% of the car's weight was sat on (or beyond) the front axle, with just 37% left to hold the back end down. In total, the quote weight for the Audi Sport quattro was 960kg (2,116lb) on its debut in Corsica, although in truth it was around the 1,200kg (2,646lb) mark.

The shortened car was incredibly nervous by nature, which proved rather a trial for its occupants. Besides its quirky weight distribution, Audi chopped the air dam of the car beneath the integral radiator and bumper, extending the composite sump guard upwards to meet it like a clam shell. The result was that the Audi's nose would be pushed upwards by the airflow, which relieved the drivers of any remaining sense of control that they may have entertained. Mikkola and Blomqvist lobbied hard to have their Quattro A2s returned.

In hindsight it was probably fortunate that the Audi Sport quattro debuted on the same weekend as the car that was to define Group B: the Peugeot 205 T16. The deficit between the Sport quattro and the Peugeot was as large as that of the rear-wheel drive Escorts and Talbots had faced against the early Audis – which meant that development had to happen swiftly.

The first response in Ingolstadt was to throw more power at the wheels, but the

ABOVE LEFT The short wheelbase Quattros used more upright A-pillars and associated panels from the Audi 80. *(Author)*

ABOVE The enlarged sump guard under the Sport quattro's needle nose generated unhelpful amounts of lift. *(McKlein)*

ABOVE The instrument panel of the rally Quattros was always a bespoke piece. This is the Group 4 version. *(Author)*

shortcomings in the car's handling would preclude going too far. Instead the whole car was re-engineered with as many of the ancillaries as possible being taken out of the engine bay and put in the boot. The radiator with its attendant fans, together with the alternator, were thrown to the rear extremities, the oil cooler relocated and the centre of the car required to accommodate roughly 10kg (221lb) of additional piping and wiring.

Its bodywork would also need to be redesigned with a raft of appendages to regain control of the little beast – resulting in the dramatic-looking Audi Sport quattro S1.

Audi Sport's engineers went to dramatic lengths to use the air to push the car down. A vast rear wing was mounted on the boot and a snowplough front wing was wrapped around the bodywork, from which long strakes reached back over the extended front wheel arches to channel the air down the sides of the car in tandem with extended door sills.

LEFT The original dashboard of IN-NX 47 shows that the Group B weight loss programme was in full swing – note the warning light, a VW Beetle indicator. *(Author)*

BELOW LEFT Any semblance of the production car's interior was eradicated on the S1 – a simple titanium tube frame on which the instruments were mounted, and a piece of cloth acting as the upper surface. *(Author)*

BELOW The interior of the S1 was a lighter, brighter place to be – plastic windows, bare panels and redesigned crash structures were purely functional. *(Author)*

Roland Gumpert claimed that the downforce generated by the new bodywork was the equivalent of 500kg (1,102lb) – with the advantage that those 500 kilos weren't physically present. The new car would have looked very composed, were it not for the extra 100+ bhp under its bonnet.

The wheelbase was also increased by 20mm compared to the Sport quattro. In this final iteration, Audi got the weight balance at 52% on the front axle and 48% at the rear, with the total weight being claimed to be 1,100kg (2,425lb).

This would be the ultimate iteration of the Quattro in all its rally forms. A mid-engined prototype was assembled – in fact four of them – after design work was commenced in mid-1984. At first this work was spoken of

BELOW Outlandish from every angle, the S1 delivered extreme performance and an operatic sound with functional aerodynamic drama. (*Author*)

ABOVE It was entirely natural for Audi to have investigated a mid-engined bespoke competition car of its own, but the S1 remains the ultimate Quattro.

(Audi AG)

ABOVE A revised S1 was used to break the 11-minute barrier for climbing Pikes Peak in 1987. Freed from the homologation constraints enforced by the FIA, it was a truly wild creation – an S1 on steroids.

(Audi AG)

openly but as official disapproval mounted, the project was moved out of the Ingolstadt factory and into a corner of the Neckarsulm plant. The mid-engine prototype was not tested until the autumn of 1986 when it was sent to Czechoslovakia for Walter Röhrl to assess.

When the FIA announced that the 1.2-litre turbocharged Group S would be phased in through 1987–88, Audi decided that its future lay elsewhere and Ferdinand Piëch demanded a halt to all activity. The three cars that were built officially were crushed under Piëch's supervision but the fourth survived and now resides with Audi Tradition with the full 2.1-litre Group B engine and the concept car bodywork rather than the truncated Sport quattro shape that it ran in 1986.

The Sport quattro S1 had one last mutation, however, for Walter Röhrl's all-out assault on the Pikes Peak International Hill Climb of 1987.

All remaining traces of the road car shell were removed from this one-off vehicle in favour of a purpose-built spaceframe dressed in Kevlar panels, with which a 50/50 front-to-rear weight split was finally achieved. The original panels were taken from the S1 with which Bobby Unser had won the 1986 event, and to the naked eye it was a near-identical car with a few additional NACA ducts. So ended the line of the original Audi Quattro.

Engine

The 2,144 cc 'WR' five-cylinder cast iron engine block of the original Group 4 cars was largely standard, but its ancillaries were optimised through 1980 to a new specification. The first requirement was reduced weight, the second was improved throttle response and finally the confection needed to be able to endure operating in extremes.

On all models from 1980–86, the engine was angled over by 27.5 degrees sloping left-to-right when viewed head-on (exactly as the road cars were). This arrangement helped to keep the front end as sleek as possible when the large inline engine was placed on top of the front wheels and drivetrain.

All of the rally engines were built by the specialists at Lehmann, who started by swapping the Bosch Jetronic fuel injection for Pierburg's old-style mechanical system's more direct approach to feeding the cylinders. Their main concern was power, and to the greater extent that meant the turbo, so the five-cylinder's compression ratio was dropped from 7:1 to 6:3:1 in order to allow for higher levels of boost.

The standard KKK K26 turbocharger was fitted to the earliest cars but, at the 1981 Swedish Rally, smaller turbines were fitted to try and reduce the ponderous throttle lag of the original system. On the road cars the intercooler was mounted next to the turbo behind the right-hand pair of headlights but on the rally cars it was moved to a central position lower down – and after the oil cooler was put on the boot lid, the available space was filled with a larger intercooler.

Run as a dry sump engine, the oil tank was placed in the boot and fabricated, along with

the fuel tank, by Matter. As with the road car, the reverse flow cast aluminium cylinder head featured hemispherical combustion chambers and two valves mounted vertically per cylinder. A new head was developed in time for the 1981 Sanremo Rallye to improve cooling.

From the 1981 Rally Portugal onwards, the standard single overhead camshaft was replaced by a new design with six bearings forged to optimise the spread of power for sharper acceleration. This first round of turbo modifications meant that the amount of available boost rose to a variable 1.5–1.8 bar.

In total, these enhancements took the standard 'WR' Quattro output of 200 brake horsepower and 206 lb.ft of torque, and beefed it up reliably to 300 bhp above 5,500 rpm and a maximum 304 lb.ft of torque, which was delivered at 3,250 rpm. By late 1981, output had risen to 320 bhp.

In order to future-proof the engine it was necessary to think ahead to when Audi Sport would start its almost endless battle to remove weight from the Quattro. To this end, a second homologation was made for an alloy version of the 'WR' block with GG cast iron cylinder liners, shaving 22kg (48lb) from the weight. This engine would be debuted on the 1982 Tour de Corse and continue into the Group B era inside the Audi Quattro A1 and A2.

The alloy engine development was led by Dr Fritz Indra, who had formerly produced such exotica for BMW's competition and high-performance division. In total, the engine design team numbered four people, as the ever-forthright Dr Indra declared that more people would just get in the way.

The A2 featured the sleeved-down cylinders to give options of 2,110 cc or 2,135 cc in order to get the Quattro beneath the 3-litre engine capacity line laid out in the regulations, which in turn allowed the car to run at a total weight of less than 1,000kg (2,205lb). The smaller engine capacity was countered by fitting a more potent turbo, the KKK K27, with either a small 12-blade turbine or larger 14-blade turbine depending upon the characteristics of the event.

This was almost as far as development would reach on the original 10-valve engine, which in 1983–84 saw 360 bhp as the standard output. From 1983 onwards, attention in the

ABOVE The Group 4 engine used Pierburg mechanical fuel injection and Hitachi engine management. A compression ratio of 6:3:1 was standard. *(Author)*

ABOVE The KKK K26 turbocharger was initially used in standard form, but soon bespoke turbines were developed to help reduce throttle lag. *(Author)*

BELOW The Group 4 engine started with 300 bhp and rose in increments to 320 bhp by the end of the 1981 season. *(Author)*

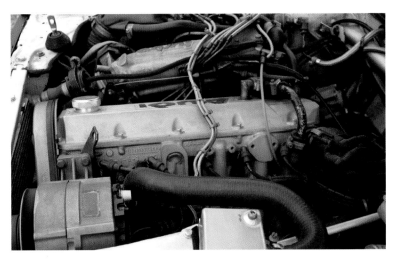

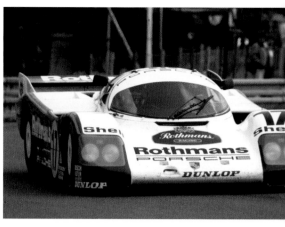

ABOVE At the end of 1982 a second homologation was granted for an all-alloy block that was developed by Dr Fritz Indra, which shaved 22kg from the weight ahead of the front axle. *(McKlein)*

ABOVE As the Group B engines evolved, they began to reflect many aspects of Porsche's turbocharged flat-6 engine. The same compression ratio, turbochargers and engine management were deployed. *(Porsche AG)*

engine shop shifted towards the new 20-valve 'KW' engine that would eventually be fitted in the short wheelbase cars. Some elements of the new engine were competition tested first on the 10-valve engines during the 1984 season, most notably a new 'Umluft' wastegate, which gave an additional 500 rpm in the optimum range and reduced throttle lag.

These were areas where the technology within the Audi Quattro began to integrate usable parts from Porsche's dominant Group C sports car, the 956 and later 962 variant. While relationships between Ferdinand Piëch and the Porsche family were seldom cordial, the two brands that they represented were able to work collaboratively to tremendous effect.

Such support was highly valuable when trying to solve the riddles of the Audi Sport quattro. Its 20-valve cylinder head and twin overhead camshafts immediately kicked available power up to more than 400 bhp. Another benefit of the new cylinder head was that the turbo was relocated away from the fuel lines, removing one of the major causes of conflagration in the early rally Quattros.

BELOW The arrival of thoroughbred Group B cars like the Lancia 037 inspired a quest for more power. To this end Dr Fritz Indra developed the 20-valve cylinder head. *(Author)*

BELOW RIGHT The 20-valve engine had the potential for devastating power, while on a practical level moved the super-heated turbo away from the fuel lines, reducing the risk of fire. *(Author)*

Until the smaller car's weight gain could be reversed, the performance from the 20-valve would be blunted. This was most clearly seen under acceleration, because the peak torque of the engine was 1,000 rpm higher up the rev counter than it was on the 10-valve, which meant a lot of the available grunt was squandered.

This is where the addition of Walter Röhrl's forensic abilities as a test driver came into their own – not to mention his close ties to the Porsche *werk*. Endless variations of wheels and transmission were tried, but the lion's share of the work fell to Bosch in getting the ECU to optimise the power and torque for the singular demands that the Sport quattro made.

Not until the start of the 1985 season were the fruits of this development programme truly revealed, when Röhrl showcased the much more usable Sport quattro, taking the lead of the Monte Carlo Rally from Peugeot and remaining in contention for victory until the very last stages. Of course, a fair degree of the performance was down to Röhrl's love affair

ABOVE The Audi Sport quattro S1 saw the removal of all ancillaries from the bonnet and placed in the boot in a bid to tame the short wheelbase handling. *(Author)*

BELOW LEFT The radiator and its colossal fans dominated the boot space of the S1. *(Author)*

BELOW The oil cooler was taken off the boot lid and placed inside to allow for the aerodynamic package. *(Author)*

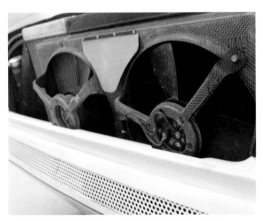

BELOW LEFT The fuel and oil tanks remained where they were, albeit somewhat less accessible. Spare wheels went inside the car. *(Author)*

BELOW The alternator was repositioned right alongside the battery. *(Author)*

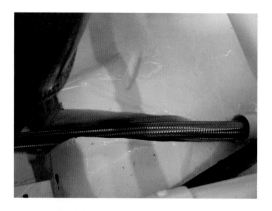

RIGHT All of the plumbing for the engine had to traverse the length of the S1 cockpit. The direct route was chosen. *(Author)*

FAR RIGHT The driver and co-driver sat atop a veritable snake's nest of pipes and ducting. *(Author)*

RIGHT The co-driver had the main arteries to the engine running down past his or her calves to feed the rapacious 550 horsepower beast beyond their toes. *(Author)*

at Pikes Peak. With only 20km (12.5 miles) to cover, this unique engine was claimed to have been putting out more than 600 bhp by Audi – but was confirmed years later by Röhrl to have been 750 bhp.

Transmission

For rally use, the transmission of the rally cars was rather rougher than the refined setup used in the Quattro road cars – indeed it was rather closer to the first A1 prototype. Much of the drivetrain would be more familiar to a military service engineer who worked on Iltis jeeps than to a suburban Audi dealership's workshop.

The front and rear differentials were connected directly to one another to give only 50/50 power distribution, which reduced the number of parts exposed to potential failure significantly. The front end had no limited slip differential, and the rear end only had a 75% slip, resulting in fairly agricultural behaviour

with the Monte, but Hannu Mikkola was not far behind.

The arrival of the Audi Sport quattro S1 then gave the team licence to throw caution to the wind. The full force of the 500+ bhp S1 remains astounding to behold, provoking sights such as Stig Blomqvist popping a wheelie as he left the start line on one stage. In Finland. On gravel.

The ultimate specification would be that used by Walter Röhrl to set a new record time

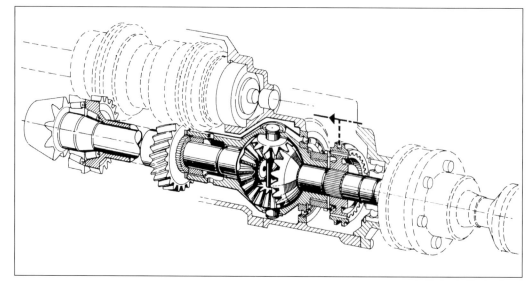

RIGHT The standard transmission layout was retained with only detail alteration throughout the Quattro's competition career. *(Audi AG)*

at low speeds, just like the very first time the system was tried out in the little red Audi 80.

The team could pick from three homologated differential ratios in the car's first iteration – 4.87, 4.55 and 4.11, mated to ratios of 3.00 for first gear, 2.00 for second, 1.50 for third, 1.217 for fourth and 1.040 for fifth. This gave the team sufficient flexibility to be competitive on all stages and surfaces (with the notable exception of Corsican asphalt), and was used through the 1981 season.

For 1982, the team did insert a central differential with 100% slip to refine the Quattro's handling. This would remain fundamentally the same system operated throughout the long-wheelbase Group B era with the Quattro A1 and A2, albeit with updated differential ratios of 4.625, 4.571 or 4.375 to choose from.

The other main addition of note came in late 1982 with an electro-hydraulic lever on the gearstick to engage and release the clutch in order to allow the driver's left foot to remain fully occupied with braking. FISA promptly banned it, but later relented. Sometimes.

The introduction of the higher-revving and more powerful 20-valve engine forced some change upon the transmission. Because of the curious problem of facing weight gains by making a smaller car it was harder to stay within the optimum rev band for peak torque, so a new 6-speed gearbox was required to help drivers to exploit the engine's full potential.

This unit was designed and built in a hurry in late 1984 and made its competitive debut on the 1985 Portugal Rally. It was discovered that the unit was running at alarmingly high temperatures so some vents were cut into the casing to try and prevent failures.

The next step to try and harmonise the car's mass, engine's power and available traction came with the addition of a Ferguson viscous coupling on the centre differential to be able to adjust the front/rear distribution. This could be locked on or off, but Audi has always kept quiet on how much power was distributed where using this system.

The 6-speed with the Ferguson differential was used to greatest effect by Walter Röhrl when he took Audi's last and hardest-won world championship victory, the 1985 Sanremo Rallye. This setup would remain the primary

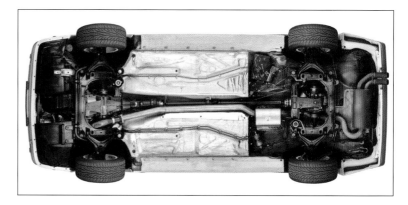

TOP Underneath the standard road-going Quattro the major components were much more exposed. *(Audi AG)*

ABOVE The delicate suspension wishbones, sump and front differential were protected by a vast panel of Kevlar on the rally cars, with a smaller version protecting the rear differential. *(Audi AG)*

BELOW A six-speed transmission was fitted to optimise the peakier 20-valve engine, resulting in a modified casing that allowed better cooling than the original, pictured here. *(Author)*

ABOVE In late 1985, Audi Sport tried out the PDK seamless transmission that had been part of the Porsche 962 development programme. *(Porsche AG)*

BELOW The forces going through the transmission in first gear are shown in blue, which would then shift to second gear, shown in green, continuing up and down the range under Bosch's electronic control. *(Porsche AG)*

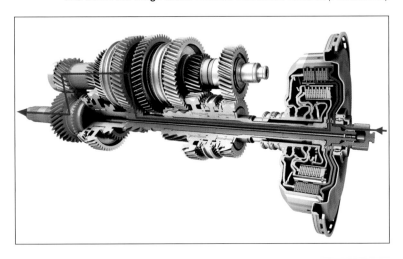

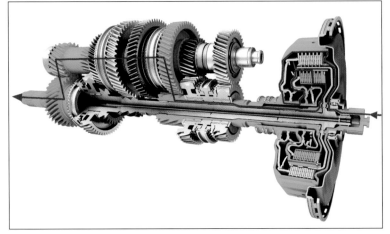

transmission layout used for the remainder of the car's competition history – although it had one last groundbreaking card up its sleeve.

In the 1960s, Ferdinand Piëch was sifting through ideas that his uncle and grandfather had come up with, looking for inspiration, when he unearthed the *doppelkupplungsgetriebe* – that had never been brought to fruition due to technological limitations of the time. The system effectively created two separate transmissions for the odd-numbered gears and the even-numbered ones. The result would be seamless gear changes, as the switch from one gearset to the other would be instantaneous.

Piëch wanted to put this arrangement into the Porsche 917 but it was still too prone to failure because it was impossible to harmonise the components hydraulically. When electronic engine management systems appeared, however, there was clear potential to adapt them for managing the intricacies of such an advanced transmission.

The Porsche *doppelkupplungsgetriebe*, or PDK for short, was never far from the top of Piëch's wish list. Its development was an integral part of Porsche's works team in the World Sportscar Championship, and Piëch encouraged greater collaboration between Audi, Bosch and Porsche to perfect the system.

When it was operating properly, PDK would allow the driver to pre-select the gear that he wanted and then concentrate on balancing the car with the throttle and/or brakes without worrying about shifting up or down. For Porsche's sports car team, the single-minded determination to develop PDK was often a frustration because its additional weight sapped performance and its unreliability cost them victories and championship points. In 1984–85, however, Audi Sport had a weapons-grade test driver who was thrilled at the chance to spend time developing the system rather than flogging from one rally to the next: Walter Röhrl.

Inside the cockpit, the driver had a simple lever to move backwards and forwards to select the desired gear that they wanted to reach. An LCD display on the instrument panel told them which gear they were currently in and which they had selected. Hammering down a flat-out section towards a hairpin would therefore mean that the screen read 5|1, and as soon as the driver got on the brakes the downshift would begin, with the ECUs of the engine and transmission operating in unison.

A traditional clutch pedal was used to engage first gear and launching the car from standstill, after which electro-hydraulic actuators handled the entire process as the driver commanded until the car was once again stationary. In time, the up/down lever used to select the desired gear was superseded by buttons on the steering wheel like those in modern semi-automatic racing transmissions.

The PDK was given its competition debut by Porsche at the end of the 1983 World Sportscar Championship season. Throughout 1984 it would run one car with a conventional gearbox and one with the PDK – often resulting in mechanical failure. It pressed on regardless in 1985 and endurance racing fans were amazed at the progress being made – although they were blissfully unaware that by now Audi was also sharing the load.

Walter Röhrl gave the PDK its rally debut in an Audi Sport quattro S1 on the 1985 Semperit Rally, a national level event which he won by 19 minutes. A Torsen Gleason centre differential was used instead of the Ferguson viscous coupling and video footage from the stages attests to the barely discernible blips in the engine note as the actuators did their thing.

Its performance was shattering and Röhrl's co-driver Christian Geistdörfer later claimed that he had struggled to maintain his rhythm on the notes without the familiar tempo of shifting going on beside him. Röhrl himself enjoys regaling the story of how Audi Sport engineer Dieter Basche, a regular alongside him during their many test sessions, lasted one trip in the PDK car before climbing out and swearing never to do such a thing again. In the end, the PDK transmission only had one world championship outing, in Röhrl's hands, on the 1985 RAC Rally.

The German detested the event as it was run 'blind' with no prior recce of the stages permitted, handing an advantage to drivers with local knowledge. Yet Audi insisted that he should give the PDK its debut outing and a local co-driver was found for him in the form of Phil Short.

Both Röhrl and teammate Hannu Mikkola (in a standard 6-speed manual S1) were delayed

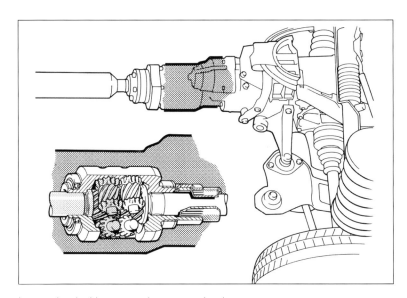

by mechanical issues and were running in eighth and ninth positions on the first night. When pushing to regain some time, with the PDK quattro now flying, Röhrl pushed too hard and the car tumbled a long way off the road.

It was always envisioned that PDK would become a standard transmission for Porsche road cars but then the idea was again mothballed. Not until 2003 would the transmission be made available to the public… in the Volkswagen Golf R32 and Audi TT, both of which were at the time under a Volkswagen group that was overseen by… Ferdinand Piëch.

No road-going Porsche went on sale with the *doppelkupplungsgetriebe* until 2009, after the company had been bought by… Volkswagen. Rightly or wrongly, one senses that there would have been considerable satisfaction among the 'non-nameholders' of the Porsche family from this turn of events.

ABOVE Torsen Gleason differential schematic. *(Audi AG)*

BELOW The PDK added weight and complexity to both the Porsche race cars and Quattro rally cars but gave shattering performance. In 2003 it reached production on the VW Golf R32. *(Volkswagen AG)*

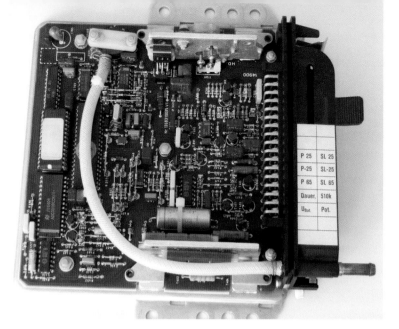

Electronics

Arguably the single greatest step in motoring
through the 1980s was the adoption
of electronic engine management. By giving
the engine a 'brain' (otherwise known as an
Electronic Control Unit or ECU), it became more
efficient, while men with laptop computers could
write programs to deliver the optimum balance
of fuel efficiency and power output.

Early ECUs would measure the load and
speed of the engine and adjust, with the data
being read by a microprocessor to then manage
the fuel flow appropriately. As the capacity of
the computers grew, so they were also able to
process information on ambient temperature,
rpm, throttle position, air pressure, and oil and
water temperature to make instant adjustments
via solenoid.

From 1980–83 the Audi Quattro rally cars used
a combination of Pierburg's fuel injection system

and a Hitachi ECU. As the Group B era began
to demand more power, higher turbo boost and
the need to fine-tune the point of ignition became
critical to engine survival. And the masters of this
art were to be found at Bosch.

The first competition department to use
Bosch Motronic engine management was
BMW, which was putting its engines under
enormous loads, both in IMSA sports-
prototype racing and in Formula 1. This was a
relatively primitive setup, with the ECU primarily
concerned with managing the mechanical
injection system, but very soon a complete
system called MP1.2 was unveiled, which was
developed initially with Ford for use with its
stillborn Escort RS1700T Group B rally car.

Both Audi and Porsche seized upon the
availability of the MP1.2 for their respective
motor sport programmes in the FIA World
Sportscar Championship and the FIA World
Rally Championship. The MP1.2 could
harmonise the amount of turbo boost required
to the speed of the engine, read the water
and intake air temperature, manage the fuel
injectors and control the point of ignition.
Initially it could only manage all of this if
there was a single injector per cylinder, but
this tended to make throttle response rather
ponderous, compounding the pre-existing
turbo lag.

When Bosch was able to upgrade the MP1.2
with two injectors per cylinder, the dreaded
throttle lag was reduced back to the same level
as it had been with a mechanical injection – but
with far greater reliability and efficiency, meaning
more power.

The final step was to fine-tune the boost
levels and throttle response by means of the
wastegate. Initially a larger capacity wastegate
from the Porsche 930 was used, in order to
maintain the speed of the turbines inside the
turbocharger when the engine revs dropped by
blowing surplus pressure outside the system.
This effectively fooled the turbo into believing
the engine was still pulling hard to ensure that
the boost remained optimal when the driver got
back on the power and reducing throttle lag.

The advent of the 20-valve engine meant
that pressures were too high for the single
wastegate to cope so a smaller second
wastegate was taken from the Porsche 944

Turbo and plumbed in between the turbo and the intercooler, which was managed by the ECU. This second wastegate was plumbed in reverse and meant that it reduced the backwards pressure when the revs dropped, dumping the gases back in to the manifold to complete a second lap of the system.

This rather complex system was called Umluft and made its competition debut on the 10-valve engines at the Portugal Rally in 1984. It was Umluft that then gave the significant increase in the volume of whooshing and popping that the high-revving 20-valve engine is famous for: as much a part of its soundtrack as the shrieking five-cylinder engine.

By the time that the Audi Sport quattro S1 appeared, the only way in which Audi could hope to make its front-engined car competitive against the bespoke mid-engined silhouette cars of Porsche, Lancia and the rest was to outgun them. This in turn reduced the system's tolerances and made engine failure a much more common problem for Audi than it was for its rivals – but when these engines were on song they were mesmerising, and could not have been achieved without the remarkable little black boxes from Bosch.

Suspension and brakes

The suspension of the rally-specification Quattros was MacPherson all round, with heavily braced steel lower wishbones. Springs and dampers came from Boge – not a supplier with much rally pedigree but one which had a lucrative commercial agreement with Audi

LEFT The combination of a large Porsche-sourced wastegate and a second smaller Porsche wastegate preventing rearward pressure resulted in the constant chittering sound that accompanied the Sport quattro and S1 at speed. *(Buffington Engineering)*

and was happy to plough some money and expertise in to the programme.

For rallies such as Corsica, the gauge of steel used, sizes of the tubes and amount of cross-bracing was pulled back to a minimum in order to help the Quattro to shed weight. For the Ivory Coast and Safari rallies in particular, the whole setup required considerable extra bracing and a granite-like feel to withstand flying over the African roads at full tilt.

At each end of the car, a steel subframe held everything in place and equally worked well for the ease of removal, repair and replacement of suspension parts at the roadside. The definitive design was in place for the 1981 Sanremo Rallye, allowing the team to switch from asphalt to gravel-specification setups in the space of five minutes.

With the arrival of significantly greater freedoms regarding materials in Group B, by mid-1982 Audi was already investigating

BELOW LEFT Boge developed the competition suspension on the Audi Quattro with competition wishbones and more robust subframes than the standard car. *(Author)*

BELOW Very early in the Quattro's rally career the definitive subframe design was reached, allowing mechanics to switch from asphalt to gravel settings in five minutes. *(Author)*

ABOVE On the 1984
Tour de Corse, former
BMW chassis expert
Dieter Basche refined
the suspension to
lower the car's centre
of gravity and improve
its ability to manage
undulations. (McKlein)

alternatives for any benefit that they might bring.
Aluminium, titanium and plastic were all built
and trialled in the construction of chassis and
suspension components. Almost exclusively,
however, the suspension retained steel arms
with aluminium fittings.

In 1985 the single Audi Sport quattro entered
for Walter Röhrl in Corsica appeared to be
much more like a racing car in its demeanour
than on any previous asphalt event. This was
a new chassis, one of two, built with input on
the suspension mounting and geometry from
Dieter Basche, the legendary BMW motor sport

engineer, who managed to shave 12mm off the
ride height while making the car suppler on the
road surface.

Great things were expected of Röhrl and the
new bespoke asphalt car – to the point that
Ferdinand Piëch was in attendance. That he
went out early in the rally was the beginning of
the end for Roland Gumpert's tenure in charge
of Audi Sport, although the retirement was due
to a bad batch of brake discs, of which two sat
broken on the front wheels of Röhrl's car.

The brakes for the Quattro were an area that
required massive and continual development.
For one thing, they were being asked to slow
30–40% more mass than the brakes of a
contemporary Ford Escort RS1800 had to deal
with and also to rein it in from a significantly
higher speed. Vented 280mm discs from AP
were fitted at the front, with 245mm discs at
the rear – the same setup and hardware as
Porsche's Le Mans-winning 935. There was
no servo assistance but the balance could
be changed from inside the car to adapt to
changing conditions and wear.

The size of the brakes did not change
considerably, even though the available power
leapt up from one season to the next. This
became a particular problem with the arrival
of the 20-valve short wheelbase cars, which
became fairly notorious for brake issues in a
very short time. At the 1984 Sanremo Rallye,

RIGHT Basche's
refinements to the
suspension continued
with the remarkable
S1, while the water
cooling for its brakes
became all-important.
(Author)

LEFT The rear of the Sport quattro S1 was
considerably heavier than previous generations,
but not until after the car's rally career was over
was a functioning handbrake available. (Author)

RIGHT On his run to the top of Pikes Peak in 1987, the differentials in Walter Röhrl's car did permit a handbrake to be used. *(McKlein)*

the Audi Sport quattros fielded for Röhrl and Blomqvist featured water injection cooling on the brakes for the first time.

For Röhrl's magnificent final world championship victory in the Sport quattro S1, the 1985 Sanremo Rallye, the water cooling was upgraded to spray an additional fine mist of water directly on to the brakes to bring them down from the critical area of 700+ degrees back down to a reliable 500+ without causing breakages.

One aspect of the brakes that was never really sorted out was a functioning handbrake. In 1982–83 one of the strengths of two-wheel drive was the ability to whip around any hairpins or tight junctions with the help of the handbrake. Because the Quattro's transmission was solid, it was simply impossible to lock the rear wheels only.

The only time in which the handbrake could potentially have been used was in the era of the final bewinged Sport quattro S1 in 1985–86, with the introduction of unlockable centre diffs. There is no evidence in the video footage of such a brake being used on a rally, but it is clear that for Röhrl's assault on the 1987 Pikes Peak there was a fully operational handbrake in place.

Wheels and tyres

In keeping with the philosophy that the road and rally cars should be as closely related as possible, the Audi Quattro started its international rally career using a choice of either Fuchs 5-spoke or Ronal 17-spoke forged alloy wheels. The Fuchs wheels were used for gravel and snow, while the Ronals were held back for pure asphalt surfaces.

In 1981–83 the wheel sizes of 6j x 15 for snow, 7j x 15 for gravel and 10j x 15 for the asphalt were retained for the Group 4 cars and the Group B Audi Quattro A1. When the more evolved Audi Quattro A2 appeared with its smaller capacity engine, this meant that wheel width would have to be reduced by an inch, taking two inches off the breadth of the Quattro's footprint – at which point the

ABOVE Fuchs wheels were generally used for gravel rallies but were produced in various widths for snow, gravel and asphalt tyres. *(Author)*

LEFT Kleber supplied the majority of factory team tyres in 1981–82 before Michelin took over. Today these modern rally tyres show the difference between gravel and asphalt tread patterns. *(Author)*

LEFT Although committed to Kleber, the factory learnt how Pirelli rubber worked through its satellite teams in Italy (pictured) and the UK, both run by David Sutton. *(McKlein)*

Fuchs and Ronal wheels were replaced for something lighter.

On asphalt, therefore, BBS was called upon to provide the Quattro's footwear, with its natty line in finned, brake-cooling discs (as also seen on Porsche's Le Mans-winning 956). On gravel, Audi elected to use the Minilite wheels that were first popularised by the BMW Mini-Cooper and had been seen on every successful Ford and Talbot through the seventies.

This combination would be retained until the start of the 1984 season, when Speedline's 5-spoke wheels would be employed on all surfaces. From the 1984 Acropolis Rally

LEFT The widest of all Quattros was the 1981 Tour de Corse specification, which looked dramatic but only added to the driver's workload at the wheel. *(McKlein)*

BELOW LEFT With the reduction in engine capacity came a change in wheel sizes, making BBS wheels the primary choice on asphalt in 1983, shown here on Lasse Lampi's car. *(McKlein)*

BELOW Fuchs wheels were retained but in 1983 it was more common to see Minilites in use on mixed or gravel surfaces. Here Mikkola famously tricycles on the RAC Rally. *(McKlein)*

onwards, there was a significant change to the snow/gravel wheel as a disc was built in to the wheel design behind the spokes to deflect rocks and the build-up of snow that might otherwise wreak havoc on the brakes and moving parts.

When it came to the tyres, Audi's first two seasons in the world championship were spent on rubber from French manufacturer Kleber which, like Boge, had no competition pedigree. Audi stated quite vehemently that its four-wheel drive would more than compensate for any deficit in tyre performance to the Pirellis and Michelins that were in use by the other teams (and that a higher degree of confidentiality could be assured).

Kleber paid a large amount of money to Audi for the association and opportunities to showcase its products through Audi's competition success, which helped the team's rising budgets. But part of the showcase involved using tyres that used the same construction as the customer product and

RIGHT Studded snow tyres were sourced from Finnish brand Timi or from Michelin. In 1985–86 they were fitted to narrow BBS rims. *(McKlein)*

this hurt performance relative to the bespoke competition rubber fitted to the Opels and Lancias, for example. The only exception to this was when Audi was running on snow in Sweden and Monte Carlo, when studded Timi remoulds of Michelin pattern were purchased – although contractually the Klebers had to go back on for the road sections between stages.

The Kleber deal was done in the days of Walter Treser. When Roland Gumpert took over the running of the technical side, he and Reinhard Rode were quick to use the national rally programmes being set up by national markets for the purposes of evaluating different types of rubber.

David Sutton built the British and Italian championship cars and fitted them with Pirelli rubber, while the Swedish championship car of Stig Blomqvist ran on Michelins. Meanwhile, across the Atlantic, BF Goodrich enrolled John Buffum's Audi USA team into its big-spending motor sport programme, once again demanding that the tyres on the rally car should have the same construction as its road tyres, just like Kleber.

Having been able to assess the qualities of all the various suppliers, Gumpert chose not to renew with Kleber in 1983 and went instead to Michelin, which would provide the works Quattros with rubber for the remainder of its front-line competition career.

Fuel and lubricants

Motor sport requires the development of motor and transmission fluids to keep pace with the performance of the cars. Then, as now, motor manufacturers tended to work with their respective global OEM lubricants provider,

as they could negotiate a good discount on the millions of litres needed for factory fill and aftermarket servicing needs.

Audi's global lubricants partnership was with Castrol and so it was the British brand that appeared on the cars... in the world championship at least. Audi UK and Audi South Africa had deals with Shell, so its branding appeared. Meanwhile Audi France had a deal with BP for fuel and lubricants, which resulted in Michèle Mouton driving a black Quattro with green and yellow stripes in 1981, and carrying the BP shield on her overalls – even when Castrol branding was on the cars.

Fuels were a different matter entirely, however. Today, a standard 'control' fuel is provided for every series except Formula 1 but the 1980s are remembered as a time of innovation in fuel composition. While the aerodynamicists and engine builders stood in the limelight, behind them were the chemists engaging in a battle unseen by the public and unheralded by the press.

The turbo era was unleashed by Porsche in 1972 under Ferdinand Piëch, inspiring BMW, then Renault, Saab and Ferrari to follow suit. As more and more power was found, and greater temperatures and pressures resulted, the problem became one of detonation – losing control of combustion and suffering engine failure as a result.

Legend has it that it was BMW engine designer Paul Rosche who, in trying to get more power from BMW's turbocharged Formula 1 engine, went to BASF and asked for the formula for fuels that had been developed for German high-altitude fighters during the Second World War. The story continues that once this special brew was mixed it was

RIGHT Fuel composition became a huge part of the turbo era led by Bernie Ecclestone's Brabham team in Formula 1 and its BASF blend from the Second World War. *(Motorsport Images)*

run on a dynamometer and 'boom!', 1,450 horsepower appeared.

The mystique of a 'Nazi super-weapon' has been part of popular culture ever since *Captain America* comics were invented, and nobody likes a good rumour better than motor sport folk. In fact, the power of the Luftwaffe's fighters was enhanced by blowing a mix of water/methanol into the supercharger when flying at low altitudes and nitrous oxide when at altitude. Alfa Romeo's supercharged grand prix cars used the water/methanol trick but there is no evidence of similar systems being used in the 1980s.

The fuel formula that BASF located was of Second World War origin and it was one of many similar blends developed by all of the fuel providers in motor sport during the turbo era. FISA specified that fuels had to be of the same octane rating as commercially available pump fuel but said nothing about their composition. The chemists laboured to come up with a very dense fuel that burned relatively slowly in the cylinders, allowing higher compression ratios, more boost and thereby more power. This was done without altering the octane rating by creating mixtures that included benzene, toluene, xylene, trimethyl-benzene and butane.

Most fuel companies prefer not to talk about their 1980s racing blends today, because the substances involved are extraordinarily harmful to humans. The heavy smell that hung over the paddocks and service areas of the time attested to their presence, however – as did the number of team members' shoes that melted if any was spilt.

Any rubber and plastic parts in between the filler neck and the exhaust would therefore need to be changed from one event to the next. Even in spite of these measures, it is widely held that Henri Toivonen and co-driver Sergio Cresto had been overcome by fumes leaking from the fuel tanks before their Lancia S4 plunged off the road on the 1986 Tour de Corse. The use of these highly specialised fuels was finally outlawed in the early 1990s.

LEFT 1980s 'rocket fuel' needed careful handling and temperature management in all major categories. Here, Shell's brew is refrigerated for as long as possible. *(Motorsport Images)*

BELOW Leaking fuel vapours from under the seats in Henri Toivonen's Lancia may have played a role in many expert opinions. Undoubtedly, the location of the tanks doomed the Finn and his co-driver, Sergio Cresto. *(McKlein)*

Chapter Five

The team's view

Behind the performance of the drivers and co-drivers lies that of their team: a travelling army that in 1980s rallying often drove the same routes as their high-profile charges. Rallies of the period were genuine marathons that lasted up to five days, upon routes reaching thousands of kilometres, which drivers, mechanics and team staff all had to cover. They were labour-intensive and majestic events that all went towards one ultimate goal: establishing the Audi brand as a global force to be reckoned with.

OPPOSITE Rallies in the 1980s were gruelling day-and-night events in which grabbing 40 winks was a preoccupation for the hard-working service crews. *(McKlein)*

ABOVE Service crews would travel en masse, leapfrogging the competitors to be ready for their arrival, with the first responding 'chase car' alongside Audi's trusty VW van. *(McKlein)*

BELOW The Quattro transmission percolated through Audi's range of cars, such as the Audi 100, which also featured an aerodynamic body as its major selling point. *(Audi AG)*

BOTTOM From a dowdy brand in the seventies, Audi became a premium player, thanks to the Quattro – this example being the personal choice of Diana, Princess of Wales. *(Silverstone Auctions)*

The be-all and end-all

To create an engineering phenomenon in motor sport requires a significant budget. Those funds not only built the cars but also fed, clothed, transported and cared for the small army of engineers, team members, drivers, co-drivers, medics, physiotherapists, PR people and sundry others who travelled as a team to each and every event. Those millions were sourced from Audi's global marketing coffers, which meant that every penny spent had to deliver a clear and measurable benefit in the sales figures.

The Audi Quattro was designed as a road car to reinvent the oft-overlooked firm that had never once, in its first 70 years, won the same renown as the giants in Germany's automotive world. The rally cars by extension had to create the image of Audi – and while the team laboured to get the cars competitive and reliable enough to conquer the competition, so did the marketing team have to work hard to turn those results into showroom success.

David Ingram was at the helm of Audi's marketing campaign in one of the most important territories that it set out to conquer: Great Britain. A passionate believer in the power of motor sport to enhance his brand's image, the revolutionary new four-wheel-drive GT and its all-star rally team were quite simply a gift from the gods.

'Quattro was the start of so much for us, really,' Ingram said. 'The cars up to that point were very high quality but very conventional, then suddenly we had a four-wheel-drive car, which previously was really only associated with agriculture, and it was a turbocharged GT car. From that we then had the aerodynamics and the 0.33 drag coefficient on the 100 and all of these things sort of came together in very short order to make people sit up and think "well, this Audi brand is actually quite interesting!"

'Much of that credit, of course, belongs with Dr Piëch,' David Ingram added. 'He couldn't or didn't want to stay at Porsche and Audi was somewhere very open-minded that supported the technical development boss with all of these unusual things that he was coming up with. It all had to get Volkswagen's sign-off but it brought the brand from nowhere, and we wouldn't have been credible selling the stuff that Audi does today without having developed it in motor sport. It gave us credibility and excitement about the technology in a way that you would struggle to achieve in any other way.'

That the Quattro rally cars were a means to a much bigger end than collecting silverware was something that every member of the teams understood. Whatever their day-to-day role was in competition, in the design or fabrication of the cars or in managing the team's fortunes on event, every single member of the squad knew that they were working for Audi's commercial success.

Phil Short was a respected competitor in his own right; a highly skilled co-driver who also took responsibility for planning the servicing of the teams competing on the world championship. 'Audi Sport as a team was technology-led simply because of the advantage that the car had, so it was ruled primarily by engineers, Roland Gumpert and Co., so that was the focus,' he said.

'But the whole idea of Audi going rallying was to show their technical prowess: *Vorsprung durch Technik*.'

Little details like fitting the cars with the same wheels as the road cars and using equipment from the same suspension company all underlined the confidence of Audi's engineers as much as it supported the marketing drive. Once the cars left the factory, however, the fortunes of the Quattro and Audi's bid for

glory fell squarely upon the men and women who were facing very different realities and challenges to those in the boardroom and marketing meetings. They were out there getting things done in the heat of competition.

The travelling circus

Rallying in the 1980s was very different to the sport that we know in 21st century. In today's World Rally Championship, events are almost entirely three-day affairs at which the teams gather in one place and stay fixed to the spot in ever-more impressive temporary structures. From these canvas castles the cars are sent out to do a loop of three or four special stages before returning to base at lunchtime, then they are sent out to do them again in the afternoon.

So it is that the cars complete around 15 different special stages over three days and, if one removes the road sections in between them, the competitive distance is seldom more than that covered by Formula 1 cars in a 90-minute blast. The teams stay put and the people who cover the highest mileage on an event tend to be the corporate guests who are shuttled from one viewing spot to another.

In the Audi Quattro's time, rallies would start in one city and move off, taking in special stage after special stage along the route. This meant

that the service crews had to be in place and ready to receive the cars somewhere out in the wilds – remote servicing – before hurrying off to reach the next destination and set up before the rally cars arrived. The result was a high-speed chase for the mechanics in their heavily laden service barges, wending their way at breakneck speed between tens of thousands of cars crammed with eager spectators, for long days and sleepless nights.

'I drove up central reservations on an A-road to get through to a remote service and the police would wave us through,' chuckled campaign veteran team mechanic, Allan Durham. 'Cars would be dragged off a stage on three wheels and round the corner to a waiting van but you can't do that anymore.'

As an example, the 1985 Lombard RAC Rally consisted of 65 special stages covering a distance of 557 miles (896km) with a further 1,622 miles (2,610km) of road sections linking them together. That compares with the 2018 Wales Rally GB, which saw 23 stages covering 197 miles (317km) with 673 miles (1,083km) of road sections.

The fleet of service vehicles primarily consisted of small but heavily laden 2-litre petrol Volkswagen LT35 panel vans, while larger parts were carried in the LT28 'Koffer' trucks. A pair of Audi Quattro road cars would also be present as the 'chase cars' for the team, tracking every move of their competition siblings and equipped with enough tools and expertise to get an ailing rally car to its next service halt.

Overhead on many events there would also be a helicopter, particularly the most remote, such as the Safari Rally or the most challenging

for vehicle access, such as Monte Carlo. Audi would take roughly 30 support vehicles to the world championship events, as would Lancia, Peugeot, Opel, Porsche, Renault, Citroën, Austin Rover and Ford, then the privateers would have ever-decreasing numbers, right down to the hardy amateurs with a few mates piled into a Transit. Life was frenetic but often fun – as recalled by Allan Durham.

'Mick Jones was a real character – one of the longest-standing team members of Ford at Boreham. I remember sitting at traffic lights in the chase car and feeling a bump behind as Mick was there just tapping the front bumper of his car up against the back bumper of mine, then slowly he'd be pushing you out past the red light into a busy intersection. He'd think this was hilarious – it was the kind of thing that happened back then.'

Keeping all this movement and potential for havoc rolling to precise locations in precise order was the job of the team's rally co-ordinator, which for the majority of the Quattro's competition career was the position held by Phil Short. Although an extremely experienced and successful co-driver in his own right, he was a man who found that he relished the opportunity to develop the schedule for such a vast troupe.

'As a co-driver you're a bit of an in-car manager so you're already, if you're doing your job properly, doing that sort of stuff anyway,' he said.

In 1981, Short was co-driver for Pentti Airikkala in David Sutton's privateer team of Ford Escorts on the British Open Championship and part of the travelling party for the Rothmans-backed team on its World Rally Championship schedule. Although Ford had withdrawn as a works team, Sutton and team leader Ari Vatanen benefitted from as much

support as Ford's dedicated motor sport division could muster, including the services of long-standing logistics man, Charles Reynolds.

'Halfway through the season, Ford started to get cold feet, firstly because they knew that the old MkII Escort was going out of production and the new one was unlikely to be a rally car,' Short remembered.

'And so, basically, coming up to the Acropolis Rally in 81, Ford said: "OK, after the Acropolis, we are going to withdraw Charles Reynolds from this particular effort." So David Sutton asked me at that point if I would be willing to understudy Charles on the Acropolis with a view to continuing on for whatever rounds of the world championship were remaining at that point.

'So I said I was fine with that and I worked alongside Charles on that event, on which the Audis were excluded because of a modification on the headlamps which was letting air into the engine bay for cooling purposes. The Audis were excluded, Ari Vatanen won and at that point he became a contender for the world championship.'

Short relished the challenge of marshalling Sutton's forces to best effect, and when Vatanen and co-driver David Richards won the title against the factory might of Talbot and the new but still-frail Quattro, his credentials were evident to all. For 1982, Sutton began its long association with Audi, and Short remained in place to manage the team's British Open campaign with Hannu Mikkola and Arne Hertz. Nevertheless, Roland Gumpert could see the benefit of Short's calm and measured presence upon a team and swiftly recruited him to bring order to the major international events as well.

'We used to do the coordination from an aircraft because of the range, rather than a helicopter,' Short said. 'The team did have a helicopter that was used from time to time by the team but the coordination for the event was done from an aircraft. It was primarily to control the movement of the service vehicles and the service areas. There would be a service schedule drawn up before the event and the service crews needed to follow that. It would take a certain amount of management while the event was live to make sure that the right people were in the right place at the right time.

'With the factory team, I did the aerial coordination in '82 for a number of rallies. Sweden stands out, New Zealand, Ivory Coast – those sort of events. As far as Audi UK were concerned we didn't have an aircraft, we just did it on the ground. I suppose initially it would be about 50/50 between coordinating events and actually competing on them.'

The core team in Ingolstadt numbered 40–45 people in most seasons, all based in the large former supermarket warehouse on the outskirts of the city. The upper decks had offices for the head of the entire operation (Walter Treser initially, Reinhard Rode succeeding him, Roland Gumpert from 1982–85 and Herwart Kreiner in 1986), together with senior staff such as homologation engineer Jürgen Bertl, head of engine development Fritz Indra and his chassis engineer counterpart Dieter Basche, together with head of press Dieter Scharnagl and, from 1982, Reinhard Rode's command post for all of the national rally programmes worldwide.

The core of Audi Sport engineering staff would be joined by whatever talent was needed to actually compete on the rallies, swelling the team numbers up to as high as 700 on occasion. Among them would be staff engaged in Audi's other rally programmes, such as Lancastrian rally veteran Allan Durham, who had been taken on to engineer the team competing in the South African national series.

As with all of Audi's staff, Durham could

expect to be called upon for several other events per year outside his main remit – usually the Ivory Coast, Safari and RAC rallies. Getting out of South Africa to attend these events was, however, a bureaucratic quagmire that Audi had to add to its myriad costs in time and money to keep the rally cars rolling.

'Because I was resident and had a resident's stamp in my passport for South Africa, I was barred from travelling to Europe or even to Kenya for the Safari,' Durham recalled. 'So what I had to do was go to Zimbabwe, go to the British embassy there, give my passport in and they would give me another to say I was resident in Zimbabwe rather than South Africa, which allowed me to travel to Kenya or Europe. Then I'd do my job and fly back to Zimbabwe, give that passport back and pick up the one with my South African residency in it to get home again! Audi Sport did all that for me – they did all the negotiations and paperwork but otherwise you really couldn't do a lot outside South Africa.'

Once the teams were mustered, they were usually straight into the thick of the action. The

LEFT After Walter Treser's removal from the team, Reinhard Rode (right) took over the administration and Roland Gumpert managed the engineering. Soon Gumpert would be in sole charge and Rode was tending to the national market team needs. *(McKlein)*

BELOW Audi Sport's factory may have been intended for rather more domestic purposes but it was an immaculate engineering house. *(McKlein)*

rally community is a close-knit and friendly place to this day, where everyone involved shares a sense of good fortune to be pursuing a job in the sport that they love. It may have been a case of no quarter being given while the stopwatch was running but the social side of rallying was every bit as important, as Durham remembered.

'Back then you'd be in the same hotels as other teams... You'd eat together, compete with each other, get drunk together. There was a lot of banter – especially coming our way because the Quattro was so dominant. Mind you, it made the other teams build some superb cars to try and catch us.'

For Durham, one event in particular stood out above the rest. 'The Safari used to go on for four days, and you would leave Nairobi and go off on different legs. Even though we were chasing and on public roads you had a bit more time, you could interact with the locals, you'd barter at water crossings and things like that. A lot of rallies went by in a blur but you got a sense of being somewhere very, very special in Kenya.'

Testing, testing

While the hordes of team staff and main flotilla of vehicles would arrive a week or two before the start, it was highly likely that the core of the team would have been on site for a lot longer. The pre-event recce for a works team was usually a four-week process, with the crews driving the entire route three times to make their detailed pace notes, work out any emergency routes to get to service halts and identify any locations that might be suitable for changing tyres or any other minor but potentially rally-winning repairs and adjustments on the fly.

The recces would be performed in road cars, usually Audi Quattros, which had a degree or two of modification to allow them to pass over the terrain, such as sump guards and raised suspension. There would also regularly be a competition car on hand for pre-event testing – a duty that became all the more onerous with the arrival of Walter Röhrl in the team.

One Quattro driver who later became a competitor to the Audi Sport team was Britain's young hope, Malcolm Wilson. In 1985 he was signed to join the Austin Rover squad to bring its Metro 6R4 to the world's elite competition and to him the luxury of Röhrl's extended pre-event routine was something from another world.

'That's why we've got restrictions on all the days of testing, etc. in the World Rally Championship today,' he chuckled.

'In those days Walter was very, very clever in the fact that he would maybe pick six, seven rallies in a year and that's all that he would do. But you could guarantee that if he picked that rally and he would do it then there was a very good chance that he was going to win

RIGHT Long before the crowds arrived, rally crews would be pounding the stages for weeks on end as they refined their all-important pace notes during the recce. *(Fred Gallagher collection)*

because, yes, he could go and practice for three weeks or six weeks if he wanted.'

For the research and development of the Quattro, however, it was often preferable to do testing far beyond the prying eyes of rival teams. Thus the appearance of a creamy-white Volkswagen LT van or three and a burbling five-cylinder rally car could be spotted at many extraordinary locations around the world, including the narrow, winding roads of Czechoslovakia, the searing heat of North Africa and the mountains around Johannesburg.

It was this need to seek solitude that ended up with Allan Durham leaving the north of England for somewhere very different indeed and a whole new life, thanks to Audi.

'A friend of mine from the local motor club in Bury emigrated to South Africa in 1980,' said Durham. 'We kept in touch and he phoned me one day and said: "You'll never guess what I've been doing…" and he told me he had been working for this big rally team, Audi Sport, that had gone to Johannesburg to do high-altitude testing on its new car.

'And he said that these lads have come from Germany and they want to run cars here in South Africa for development and they're looking for mechanics. He said, "You should apply", and he sold me completely on the lifestyle down there, so I got in touch with the factory.

'In those days in South Africa everything was done on the quiet. Nobody really wanted to know what was going on there because of Apartheid and it was still a place that was not talked about. But they had a very good rally series. All the big teams and drivers came out on the quiet and eventually I got this job with Audi Sport. They arranged travel and visas and accommodation and everything, I packed

LEFT Far away from prying eyes, Audi's team in South Africa ran its own programme and developed components that would be fitted to the works cars, once homologated. *(Allan Durham collection)*

RIGHT Work to do on this one! Allan Durham is first on the scene when driver and team principal Geoff Mortimer takes an unintended diversion. *(Allan Durham collection)*

these parts come back for us to put on our cars. And they really were the be-all and end-all, so it was nice to be involved in that side of it.'

Furnishing the teams with helicopters and aeroplanes, juggling diplomatic requirements for travelling team staff and sending freshly made components to outposts around the world was all meat and drink to the daily operation of Audi Sport. At its peak, the team operated on a budget of £3.5–4 million in its push to win the 1983–84 world championship titles (£12–14 million today) in seasons of 12 events. That's more than double the budget of a manufacturer running three cars on 14 events in 2019.

Part of the funding came from the income from Audi's national rally programmes buying cars and needing to service them, while part came from supplier deals with the likes of Castrol, Recaro and Boge. In 1984 the Audi Sport team finally bit the bullet and took a title sponsorship from HB Cigarettes, a brand of British American Tobacco, which helped to offset the development of the Sport quattro and its S1 evolution. From the perspective of a team owner today, however, the level of extravagance seen by the big teams of the 1980s has something of a dream-like quality to it.

'That's part of history now,' said Malcolm Wilson, whose M-Sport team has been the focal point of Ford's global rally programme since the late 1990s, winning the 2006 manufacturers' championship with the Ford Focus and then back-to-back drivers' titles in 2017–18 with Sébastien Ogier in the Fiesta WRC.

'If it was still like that the costs would be… I remember in that era the manufacturers and the people who were competing, they weren't restricted by budgets like we are nowadays. I mean, it was just a case of if a manufacturer decided "Well, we're going in the World Rally Championship" then my impression, I don't know all the ins and outs, but the impression that you got as a driver then was that, well, if Audi or Ford or whoever is going in to rallying they're going to spend whatever it takes to do the job. Whereas nowadays, you know, that just couldn't be the case because you can imagine, the way that technology is, it just could run completely wild. That couldn't work in this current day and age, the budget then required to do things like that would just be astronomical.'

ABOVE Drivers would often cause mechanics sleepless nights – Michèle Mouton had them busy with hammers and tape after this excursion. *(McKlein)*

BELOW The modern WRC is a much leaner, less costly form of motor sport than its ancestor of the Quattro's time – although that community spirit remains intact. *(Ford Motor Company)*

up everything here and with the wife and two children we just went: that was that.'

In the vanguard of Audi's South African team was Sarel 'Supervan' van der Merwe, a second-generation competition driver whose father had run a DKW dealership in the week and campaigned the company's cars in competition at the weekend. Having proven himself to be a rare talent on the track and rally stages against visiting stars from around the world, van der Merwe was to lead Audi's competitive outings in South Africa while also testing new parts for the Ingolstadt team.

'We did quite a few things like that and they were so good,' said van der Merwe. 'They would say test this thing and compare, or test that thing and compare, and not everything worked. Sometimes it made things worse, but we gave them the feedback and eventually we would end up seeing the proper homologated version of

RIGHT David Ingram was responsible for making Audi UK's team, run by David Sutton and employing star drivers like Hannu Mikkola, deliver in terms of dealership success. *(McKlein)*

Far away from Ingolstadt

From 1982 onwards, the Audi Quattro phenomenon began to spread out around the world in hugely successful national and regional rally championship campaigns. In Europe, Schmidt Motor Sport returned to the fold in order to run a team in the FIA European Rally Championship, the German national rally championship and the Austrian series. David Sutton was engaged to prepare entries in the British Open Rally Championship, the Italian Rally Championship and the Finnish Rally Championship.

'We ran Hannu in the Audi UK car in the 1982 British championship and that took the car from the TV audience for rallying out into the country itself,' remembered Audi UK marketing chief David Ingram.

'The philosophy was to develop the car and that markets would then run it in their own championships. They provided the technology and we provided the wherewithal to do it. Audi had already been speaking to David Sutton and so Sutton's team was entrusted to build a UK car down in Ingolstadt at the end of '81 and bring it back to the UK and run it in the British championship. We had technical support always from Germany but British guys running it on the events.'

Ingolstadt was nevertheless extremely cautious in where it placed its cars and who would get the opportunity to run them – hence the multiple series in which Schmidt and Sutton would operate. The intellectual property contained within the Quattro was simply too valuable to start throwing around towards teams who may well defect to another manufacturer, taking its secrets with them.

RIGHT Malcolm Wilson built his reputation as a driver and a team operator with the ex-Audi UK Quattro, seen here restored to its 1984 glory. *(Bonhams)*

ABOVE Schmidt Motorsport ran the majority of European programmes for Audi, such as Marc Duez's Belga-backed assault on the 1983 European Rally Championship. *(McKlein)*

There was also the incentive of keeping a clean balance sheet to think of internally.

'Ingolstadt was run in such a way that they wouldn't sell anything to keep money there,' Allan Durham remembered. 'When they did their annual audit it looked like they had no end of money. There was a lot of stuff sitting in cages that you could have sold to teams or built a lot of cars out of them and sold them but they just wouldn't. It would make the figures look bad, so it was just held on there.

'If you were a privateer team you couldn't really hope to run the Quattro because Audi wouldn't release the parts unless you were associated with the brand directly. Sutton had the exclusive rights in the UK so if you wanted a car, like Malcolm Wilson, you'd have to go through him to get everything.'

Going through David Sutton was exactly

what Malcolm Wilson chose to do after his employers at Ford cancelled the Escort RS1700T programme. Although he was still part of Ford's operation, Wilson chafed at the lack of competitive seat time that he was getting at what was a critical juncture in his career – so he decided to take matters into his own hands. After David Sutton had run Hannu Mikkola in 1982 and then dominated the 1983 season with Stig Blomqvist, the talented Cumbrian put everything on the line to get his hands on the German supercar.

'Okay, I put my life savings to be honest into buying Stig's British championship winning car from '83,' Wilson remembered.

'I bought the car from Audi Sport UK, which was being run by David Sutton, and in all honesty that is the car that basically reignited my career and put me into the position to get the offers of the factory drives that I had for the 1986 season.'

Until that point, Malcolm Wilson Motorsport had been a team like many others in the domestic British scene, working with the simple and lightweight Ford Escorts that predominated in most events. Even with the support of David Sutton to guide him, the prospect of the Quattro as something to tinker with in the garage was a daunting one:

'You can imagine all we'd ever done was MkII Escorts, that was all we'd ever run,' Wilson said.

'You're absolutely right, it was a big technology change from our side and from myself basically going from carburettored engines to Pierburg fuel injection, four-wheel drive… it was a massive step. But I think, in fairness, by the end of '83 the car had been reasonably reliable – OK, there was a weak link in the transmission and things especially on tarmac – but in all honesty it was a much easier car to run than probably what we envisaged.'

In 1985, another stalwart of the British rally scene, Andy Dawson, also got his hands on a pair of Audis – this time direct from the factory. British American Tobacco was breaking into the vast Chinese market with its 555 cigarette brand. To make a big impression in China, it was going to use motor sport to advertise its products.

'They said: "We have agreed to sponsor the Hong Kong–Beijing Rally, and the first entries

we've got are all sponsored by Marlboro. Help! What suggestions do you have to make sure that a 555-sponsored car wins the rally?"'

Dawson was enrolled to help find a solution, and having failed to convince any of the major teams to swap to a 555 sponsorship offer, he knew that a different direction was needed.

'About the fourth call that I made was to Arwed Fischer, who co-drove for me in the Datsun when I did the German rally championship and he was by now competition manager at Audi. So I explained the situation to him and he thought that the three months that I had to get a solution for BAT was mad. Anyway, he came back with the figures for two cars and for Hannu to drive one of them.'

Dawson presented the figures to BAT and the prospect of having the world-beating Quattro on their side was too good to miss. The budget was high, but the returns of success in the world's biggest market dwarfed them in comparison. 'If I remember correctly the money was in my bank account by the time I got home from Weybridge,' Dawson chuckled – and he headed straight to Ingolstadt to start a ten-day mission to buy and prepare one Quattro for the team's unveiling.

'I paid 85,000 quid for it and I had a trailer there the following day to pick it up and bring it back,' said Dawson.

'A week later I drove it up to the BRDC suite, painted yellow, to announce to the 555 Rally Team. I drove it up from Competition Coachworks, where it had just been finished off, driving up the lane and there was a big puddle there so I drove it through the puddle with the money man from BAT sitting beside me. We took a picture and that became a poster!'

There were one or two members of the rally community who were taken by surprise when the event sponsor announced that it was going to field Quattros, particularly with one car to be driven by Hannu Mikkola. The Toyota, Opel and Nissan teams had expected to battle for the win between themselves, while closer to home there were also some stern questions asked.

'I remember David Sutton was livid because we announced the deal at Silverstone and he got on to Audi UK, then Audi UK got on to me and said: "David Sutton has the exclusive rights to rally the Quattro in the UK." And I said: "Fine,

but we're not going to rally the car *in* the UK!"

'Anyway, I explained all this to BAT and they just went: "Well, *we'll* buy the cars for you to run them!" So BAT paid for it, I got Audi to rescind my invoice and do up another invoice to their sponsor, HB Cigarettes, which was also a BAT brand, and that sorted all the problems out there and then – job done and thank you, Mr Sutton!"'

The rally was to be a 2,200-mile (3,540km) dash over four days and nights from a ceremonial start in Hong Kong to the finish line in Tiananmen Square. Having committed to sending its Quattros out into the unknown, Audi then weighed in with support to Dawson's highly skilled but small-scale team, including feeding, clothing and transporting numerous members of its own staff – among them Allan Durham.

'Before the rally, Andy did a press day in Hong Kong and blew the engine,' Durham

LEFT Allan Durham and the team received a replacement engine in Hong Kong and had it running with only minutes to spare before the event. *(Allan Durham collection)*

BELOW The 555 Rally Team wanted for nothing in terms of logistical support, seen here at base camp in a Hong Kong car park. *(Allan Durham collection)*

recalled. 'There wasn't another engine available in Germany; the only one that was available was a rallycross engine that Lehmann had sitting on his dyno, so they said "it's that or none."

'Everything had already been shipped to China so we got the rallycross engine. We got it about 9pm or 10pm on Saturday night and the rally started at 8am the following morning! So there we were in an underground car park in Hong Kong, in 100% humidity, removing the broken engine and getting the new engine in. We just got it in, finished, up and running and the car went straight from there onto the start, and I think there were 15 minutes to spare.'

All of this meant that Dawson's introduction to rallying an Audi Quattro was a little less inspiring than he had hoped. 'My car that I drove was like a Foden tractor in comparison [with Mikkola's],' he laughed.

'Mine had an old turbo with a lot of lag on it and it had the rallycross engine in it so you could never get to use the power anyway. You'd push the accelerator down and by the time that the turbo woke up and did anything it was time to change gear!'

Despite these issues, both of the Quattros made it off into the wilderness of a country that had closed its borders to the West in 1949 and only just opened them a crack for pop band Wham! to play the first pop concert in its history earlier in the year. Rather than being offered the red carpet treatment, however, the rally crews and their entourage would simply have to hurtle along the largely unpaved roads as fast as they could – including Allan Durham.

'The people, you'd see them out in the sticks and they'd never seen Europeans before,' he recalled. 'We were getting prodded and poked. We drove through some villages and people were throwing chickens in the road as we were going by so they dinged off the car. It was weird!

'The guy I was with was called Simon Everitt, a rally driver, and the idea was that we would go in the chase car. He would be the main driver, I'd co-drive him and we'd be the first on hand when the cars stopped. Anyway, he ate something before we left Hong Kong and the first day out he got really violently ill, and I just strapped him in the passenger seat and I was driving and co-driving and wondering what the hell am I going to do with this poor bloke? I thought he might die on me, and there we were flying through the countryside in the middle of nowhere getting chickens thrown at us!

'The rally was in sections and they had trucks along the route with fuel. Everybody had to pull up and hand pump the fuel off these trucks and then continue – the timing was running all the time.

'We left this one place at 8pm and Hannu set off, then I set off and was maybe ten minutes behind him. And we chased the whole night. We stopped at fuel trucks on the way and continued, and we got to the end through control and Hannu was sitting on a grass bank at the side of the road – he'd been sat there over an hour!

'I only left ten minutes after him and I thought I was pushing hard through the night. We were catching cars and passing cars, everyone was on the same route – service vehicles, chase cars, rally cars – all together. I've got no idea how he did the time he did. It made me realise that the rally driving I'd done early in my career was a little bit tame!'

Also keeping the British end up was Andy Dawson, who had by now overcome the less-than-perfect properties of his engine to come bounding up through the field.

'I will always and forever remember going across the plains in China, and we had got the cars geared up to the highest gearing we could get in them, so 155 mph [250kph], and we were on the rev limiter for miles and miles in fifth,' he said.

BELOW Throughout the epic route, the arrival of Western rally cars drew enormous interest from the local communities, many of whom had never seen foreigners before. *(McKlein)*

'I was on one of those straights and remember seeing a jump, a bridge, and I went over it and the damn thing didn't jump straight because the left-hand track rod and the right-hand track rod are different lengths. So they bump-steered differently one side to the other. It was a fast, fast rally that one.'

Eventually, Hannu Mikkola and Arne Hertz crossed the finish line, just over six-and-a-half minutes in front of the Nissan 240 RS crewed by Lars-Erik Torph and Hans Thorzelius, with Dawson finishing just seconds off the podium in fourth. At dawn on the fourth morning, the convoy passed through the archway in the Great Wall of China into the nation's capital to park in Tiananmen Square: mission accomplished. Dawson would return in 1986 with his 555 team, with which Stig Blomqvist and Bruno Berglund would take the Quattro's second and final win in the Chinese marathon.

Endgame

Once its many early gremlins had been contained, the Audi Quattro's primacy lasted for two-and-a-half seasons in 1982–84 before the arrival of the Peugeot 205 T16 ushered in a new era. These lightweight mid-engined cars were quick to make the Quattro appear leaden in comparison, and even the short wheelbase cars struggled to stay on terms.

'Put it this way: if Audi was starting with a clean sheet of paper in 1982–83 they would have designed a completely different car from what they were rallying,' said Phil Short.

ABOVE Journey's end: after four sleepless days and nights of flat-out motoring, the Hong Kong–Beijing epic ended in victory for Audi and Hannu Mikkola, beneath the unblinking gaze of Chairman Mao. *(McKlein)*

'The Peugeot and the Lancia were clean sheet designs, albeit clothed with something that was a little bit like a production car that they made. That was a significant difference, but once they got all of the problems ironed out of the specialised cars, the writing was on the wall for the Audi.'

To this day, there is a note of something approaching indignation in Audi's official stories of the Group B era: that perhaps the other manufacturers had been reading a different rulebook. Despite the very obvious disadvantage that the Quattro was carrying into

BELOW Group B allowed manufacturers freedom to create pure competition machines. This Peugeot 205 Turbo 16 shares no common parts with the road car fore or aft of the driver's seat. *(Author/Coventry Transport Museum)*

ABOVE The Quattro gave Audi a genuine story to tell – the cars that you could buy were essentially the cars competing on the rallies. And tell it Audi did, through comprehensive press material. *(Author/Guy Clinch)*

BELOW Legend has it that the mid-engined concept was completely secret. In reality it was just a logical extension of the competition programme. *(Audi AG)*

battle with the bespoke racers, the ultimate aims of selling Audis came before any mere matters of competition in the field.

'It was fundamental that the relationship between the competition car and the road car was maintained,' said David Ingram.

'It was a core element that for someone to see the rally cars winning, to read about it in the press or see it on TV at the weekend, they should know that they could go down to their local dealership and buy a car like that. Later on, of course, it could be a car with the same technology, be that an 80 quattro or a 200 quattro – and nobody else in rallying could say that.

'You couldn't realistically buy a mid-engined Group B rally car, and if you bought one of the homologation cars you probably wouldn't use it to go to the office or take the kids to school! It brought a new audience to Audi, obviously in small numbers to start with, but it was a very influential audience who then drew more people to the brand; it was a hugely powerful

marketing tool. Audi is still synonymous with rallying today and most people, they may not even have been born then, but they know exactly what a Quattro rally car is.'

By those very clear parameters, the Audi Quattro's demise was all-but a foregone conclusion, as Phil Short put it: 'In a way it was "job done" by the mid-eighties.'

Today, fans of the era still like to chew over the possibilities of the mid-engined prototypes that appeared in secret late in 1986 – although whether they were ever as mythically secret as has been reported is a moot point.

'We heard about the mid-engined car, but that was just a research project,' said Allan Durham. 'It may have been developed but it was very much just a research vehicle and by that stage within Audi everyone was looking towards going racing and leaving all this rally stuff.'

Not quite everyone, mind you. Group B may have reached the end of its life and Group S was killed off, but the rise of production-based Group A rallying brought new opportunities. Audi Sport in Ingolstadt produced a Group A version of the 200 quattro saloon car, which proved a surprise to many on its disappointing debut in Monte Carlo but bounced back to score the brand's final world championship win on the Safari.

In Britain, Audi UK also kept on pounding round the forests with Group A cars. 'Rallying had been so good to us in the UK that we wanted to hang onto it,' David Ingram remembered.

'We could see that the writing was on the wall because Audi in Germany was already gearing up to go racing in America and we were discussing what the best way forward would be before the end of 1986, that's for sure. We continued with David Llewellyn in the Group A cars but the factory was really focused on America with the Trans-Am and IMSA series and that was too far away really. We couldn't get the cars over to show people what they were and there was nowhere to run them, and really we needed a UK programme.'

Audi went all-out to impress America by putting highly evolved versions of the rally engines into spaceframe cars with four-wheel drive – exactly the same trick that had been pulled on them in Group B! The silhouette Audi 200 quattro with its 10-valve engine dominated Trans-Am in 1987 and was promptly banned,

so Audi went to IMSA with the 20-valve engine in a replica 90 quattro and repeated the trick.

Having shown the Americans what quattro was all about, Ingolstadt's eye turned homewards and to the DTM touring car series – traditionally the hunting ground of lightweight BMWs and powerful Fords. It used the V8 quattro 'limousine' and turned the car's immense mass to its advantage, crowding out the little BMW M3s to dominate once again. This was something that Audi UK and others wanted to be part of, too.

'On a fairly regular basis after Group B we were talking about when Audi would be back into touring cars and put us back on a big stage again,' said David Ingram.

'In terms of the profile of the series, the great TV coverage and the general promotion behind it, we wanted to be in British touring cars and that resulted in the A4 quattro, which followed the rally Quattro in many ways in that it was developed centrally and then we in the markets could then run the cars.

'We went into it with a big hospitality programme, national advertising, a dealer event local to each circuit in the week prior to the event with at least one driver, a team member and someone from Audi to meet and greet customers, fleet buyers, local media and everyone. We had show cars circulating the country and the BTCC

ABOVE LEFT Audi UK continued rallying into the Group B era with the production-based Group A Coupé quattro, crewed by David Llewellyn and Phil Short. *(McKlein)*

ABOVE Audi Sport campaigned the turbocharged 200 quattro in 1987, which delivered the team's final victory on the Safari Rally. *(Audi AG)*

BELOW With a highly modified 10-valve engine and a spaceframe chassis, Audi's four-wheel-drive silhouette car destroyed the opposition in Trans-Am racing in 1987, being banned at the end of its only season. *(Audi AG)*

RIGHT After dominating North American IMSA racing with the 20-valve 90 quattro silhouette cars, Audi Sport returned home to win the DTM with its remarkable V8 quattro 'limousines'. *(Audi AG)*

ABOVE The British 2-litre formula for touring cars took off around the world, leading to accessible national campaigns and huge audiences. In 1996, seven national championship titles fell to the A4 quattro, including the prestigious British Touring Car Championship. *(Audi AG)*

ABOVE Audi abandoned four-wheel drive in 1999 in order to go to Ferdinand Piëch's old hunting ground at Le Mans – and it dominated the event. *(Audi AG)*

BELOW After winning with petrol engines and diesel engines, Audi's four-wheel-drive diesel-electric hybrid brought still more domination and proudly carried the quattro name. *(Audi AG)*

became a proper part of everybody's life. It was terrific and it ran really well.'

Having sated the appetites of its national markets, winning seven different national championships in 1996, the Audi A4 quattro began to be hit by some extraordinary handicapping to bring parity for the other manufacturers. Audi's motor sport division was already looking elsewhere for its next global 'wow moment' and decided to go all-out for victory at Le Mans, the birthplace of Ferdinand Piëch's reputation at what was a critical moment in Audi's evolution.

Today and tomorrow

'I think it's fair to say that there has always been an aspect of looking at the rules and seeing where there is an advantage,' David Ingram said of Audi's 40 years in motor sport.

'Just look at Le Mans – direct injection for the early R8 then diesel technology and hybrid technology has been Audi still keeping *Vorsprung durch Technik* very much in mind and applying it to the competition vehicles as well as the road vehicles.'

From the Audi Quattro rally cars until recent times, there was indeed a very clear pattern of developing a unique solution, deploying it mercilessly and then moving on. Or as one brand management guru put it: the ideal business model.

Just as it was intended, the Quattro and its rally programme propelled Audi into the stratosphere and gave Ferdinand Piëch a landmark success from beyond the Porsche family name. He swiftly rose from heading Audi's technological innovation to heading the entire company, and as Audi grew through the 1980s into the 1990s he made it to the top of the entire Volkswagen empire.

Porsche, meanwhile, had suffered a severe contraction in its business when the economic boom of the 1980s turned into the protracted recession of the 1990s. Its fight back to profitability under combative CEO Wendelin Wiedeking often saw him lock horns with Piëch, who knew that despite his distaste for the Porsche family, the technical collaboration between Volkswagen and Porsche was the key strength of both houses.

Piëch's battle with Wiedeking enraptured the German financial media as the gun-slinging Porsche boss first tried to sell his firm to Ford (thereby ending the collaboration with VW) and then tried to buy Volkswagen. 'Either I'm shot dead, or I win,' Piëch famously said at the time.

In the end, Volkswagen bought Porsche and Wiedeking was fired. After 34 years, dominion over both Porsche and the global automotive industry became Ferdinand Piëch's alone and through his efforts, the Volkswagen Group stood tall over Daimler-Benz, BMW, Ford and all the rest.

Unfortunately for Piëch, his time on the throne was not to lead to *Pax Romana* across this empire. An attempted coup by Volkswagen CEO Martin Winterkorn grew increasingly ugly until somebody somewhere tipped off the authorities in America that VW diesels had been programmed to fool emissions testing. The emissions scandal cost Volkswagen billions in a catastrophic defeat for all of the players. The governments of Europe and the USA were out for blood, and both Winterkorn and – after considerable encouragement – Piëch reluctantly fell on their swords.

The post-Piëch culture at Audi is clearly demonstrated in motor sport's fall from grace. When Audi launched its range-topping RS5 in 2017, the ad campaign featured the car – its quattro nameplate removed, but assuredly a four-wheel-drive GT – standing still on a drag strip while a racing car hurtled off beside it. The campaign slogan was: *Nothing to prove.*

Today, Audi's competition programme revolves around the Deutsche Tourenwagen Masters touring cars and all-electric Formula E racing. Both are categories in which most of the technology is prêt-à-porter: Audi's racing cars share common chassis, transmissions, suspension, aerodynamics and much of their motor design with their competitors and thus

ABOVE LEFT Ferdinand Piëch's rise to domination of the German automotive industry began with the quattro and was complete 30 years later. His time in the sun would not last long, however. *(Audi AG)*

ABOVE In the post-Piëch world, Audi is a much less ambitious brand, which is happy to compete with off-the-shelf technology in the DTM. *(Audi AG)*

cost little to run, but equally they prove nothing of significance.

The most popular cars around the world that are carrying the four rings are those of Audi Tradition: Ferdinand Porsche's Auto Union grand prix cars and Ferdinand Piëch's Audi Quattros. Audi Tradition tops the bill at motoring events the world over, mystifying new generations with the performance, the riotous soundtrack and the technical brilliance that created these inestimable cars.

Rumour has it that Audi might return to Le Mans with a hydrogen project sometime around 2022. A return to developing groundbreaking technology is long overdue and if it comes to pass you can be certain of one thing: such a car will carry the quattro name.

BELOW Formula E offers almost a complete vehicle for manufacturers to promote their electric cars and host nations like Saudi Arabia to promote their vision of a cleaner future. Audi won the series at its first attempt. *(Audi AG)*

Chapter Six

The driver's view

'It's a shame rally sport is no longer so popular, especially for young people. It is the best teacher for correct car driving. For a young rally driver, he must know that if he is playing the hero, the tree and ditch is not going to disappear. But race drivers for the past 20 years have said: "Oh, we need more space for our mistakes!" I have done Monte Carlo in 1973 with 150 horse brakes, and in '86 with 575 horse brakes. It was the same ditch, the same tree. That is the reason why I don't like racing…' – Walter Röhrl.

OPPOSITE In rallying, the combined efforts of the driver and co-driver together forges success for their manufacturer – and an unforgettable spectacle for the followers. *(Audi AG)*

ABOVE AND ABOVE RIGHT Before the Audi Quattro, game-changing cars included the BMC Mini-Cooper and the Ford Escort, which allowed the best drivers the platform to showcase their skill. Audi followed this great tradition. *(Author)*

First impressions, lasting impressions

Throughout the first half of its front-line career, the Audi Quattro gave its drivers the thing that everyone who pulls on a helmet dreams of: the unfair advantage. Any driver's results are only as good as the car allows them to be, and while they themselves might find a crumb of satisfaction from making a poor car finish higher than it should, moral victories do not make a career.

It is also true to say that the Quattro was never the easiest of cars. It took on an air of mule-like intransigence when presented with the tortuous asphalt stages of the Tour de Corse, an event that highlighted its deficiencies against both the best two-wheel-drive cars and the later generation of Group B machinery. Yet with every driver who came into contact with the car in its heyday, there is a residual affection.

'It's a little like talking about your favourite dress,' Michèle Mouton said, reflectively. 'Sometimes it's not the right material, sometimes it's not the right colour. But it's still your favourite dress.'

Malcolm Wilson gambled every penny that he had on funding the purchase of a Quattro when his allegiance to Ford had left him facing a long spell without a competitive drive. 'I think it was a landmark for re-establishing my career, that was the big thing because that's what really then got me back into the Group B era of having the opportunities to drive for Austin Rover and Ford,' he said.

RIGHT Four-wheel drive was the 'unfair advantage' of which competition drivers dream: the means to give themselves the best chance of victory. *(Audi AG)*

As the sun was beginning to set on the Quattro's front-line career, a handful of drivers in less glamorous series managed to come by ex-works cars and put them to work with considerable success. Among them was 'Jigger' – the pseudonym adopted by Greek shipping billionaire Giannis Vardinogiannis, who claimed his national title at the wheel of an Audi Quattro A2.

'Without doubt, the quattro was a revolution in rallies, an era ended and a new era started with the four-wheel-drive revolution,' he said.

'The Quattro changed the image and name of Audi. Audi escaped from being a normal car and became a supercar. But to win – 100% of the people involved made it happen.'

For every driver who got themselves behind the wheel of the Quattro it is a matter of pride that they played a part in the transformation of Audi's image. It was a promotional tool, pure and simple, a means to the end that Ferdinand Piëch had set out to achieve – but equally it gave their experience and their careers a boost and allowed them to experience a whole new era in their sport taking shape around them.

'My father used to race DKWs as well, and, in fact, the first motor sport trophy that I got was also in a DKW in 1967. This year it's my 52nd year of competing in motor sport and, like you said, it's mostly been racing with four rings on the front,' said multiple South African rally champion, Sarel van der Merwe.

'The rally cars actually put the road cars on the map, because Audi wasn't a very strong name before the rally programme began. And, I think, even today Audi's got a very good name in the country at the moment, it's one of the top three, and even today I think that is still because of the rally programme.'

Mastering the Quattro

Getting to grips with a revolution can present problems. Prior to the Quattro the predominant layout was for the traditional front-engine, rear-wheel-drive machinery that represented the bread-and-butter models of most manufacturers, from sexy little Lancias and big boulevard cruisers like the Mercedes SLC to the tough and rorty Ford Escorts and Fiat 131s.

ABOVE Sarel van der Merwe was a world-class race and rally driver whose skills carried Audi to successive South African rally titles. *(Allan Durham collection)*

BELOW Stig Blomqvist remains the fans' favourite Quattro driver, for the sheer spectacle of watching a man content to make an understeering car bend to his will. *(Audi AG)*

Very few alternatives to this layout had become popular over the years, but when they did they had made an impact. The front-engine, front-wheel-drive Mini-Cooper famously went giant-killing through the mid-1960s, then rear-engined exotica from Porsche and Alpine had taken up the running into the 1970s before the mid-engined Renault 5 Turbo and Lancia Stratos took the rally world by storm.

Whatever their layout, two-wheel-drive cars shared a mix of lightweight, lockable rear wheels to change ends at will and the capacity for a driver to really express themselves at the wheel. As Ari Vatanen said of the Escort in which he shot to fame: 'I felt as if I was the painter, who expresses his joy of life by painting.'

One thing that is common with drivers' experiences of the Quattro is that nobody gets poetic about its handling. Arguably, the one man who did attain Vatanenesque levels of serenity in the Quattro was Stig Blomqvist, whose history of urging front-wheel-drive Saabs through the forests at improbable speed was the perfect preparation for life at Audi Sport. Although he has never been one to share Vatanen's prose style, the relish with which Stig speaks about the Quattro's prowess still shines.

'At first it was difficult to understand the amount of traction it had out of corners – it was amazing. Some people complained about understeer, but I had come from front-wheel-drive cars and it was the same problem there,' he said.

'When you have that traction in that car it is so nice. I like the feeling when I get into the Quattro. You feel everything is so easy.'

The man who led the Quattro into the field was, of course, Hannu Mikkola, a man whose skills were sought out by Walter Treser because they were a closer fit to the handling of his car than anyone else at the time. Mikkola experienced the Quattro's evolution from a pre-production prototype to the very last of the breed, whistling and popping its way towards 600 brake horsepower.

'The Quattro compels its pilot to drive with advance planning,' he said. 'One must get used to this. In practice, I particularly look for bends that tighten, but otherwise I have the situation under control with the left-foot braking.

'One of the nicest cars I ever drove was the BDA Escort. I loved it. But for my favourite this question has to be answered by the S1 Quattro. The Escort was fun, but Quattro was so much faster.'

Not every inductee to the Quattro school of motoring approached the job with the same level of bravura, however. For Malcolm Wilson, the first opportunity to drive a Quattro in anger came on the 1982 RAC Rally, when he took the wheel of LYV 4X, the David Sutton-built car that Audi UK had run in that season's British Open series.

Although a star in Britain in his own right, Wilson was among the many who had been raised on the Ford Escort's tail-wagging exuberance and eager-to-please engine. This

RIGHT After Audi's withdrawal from the world championship in 1986, Hannu Mikkola performed all sorts of odd jobs, including setting a record at Shelsley Walsh Hill Climb that lasted more than 20 years.
(Audi AG)

RIGHT Michèle Mouton adapted to the quirks of the Quattro to break records and boundaries with aplomb, comparing the car to a 'favourite dress'. *(McKlein)*

CENTRE For Malcolm Wilson, the first taste of four-wheel drive was his appearance with Audi UK on the 1982 RAC Rally. There would be many victories that followed. *(McKlein)*

meant that becoming fluent with the Quattro would need plenty of patience.

'It's fair to say initially I found it quite difficult – very difficult to be honest because of massive amounts of turbo lag on the early model. I mean, okay, the four-wheel drive was fantastic but on the other hand it was also quite agricultural in the sense with a solid centre diff, etc.

'And then of course with all that weight overhanging the front wheels… in all honesty it needed a completely different technique to anything I'd been used to and I'd never really driven much front-wheel drive. I'd driven the little Escort RS1600i but of course that had predominantly reacted like a front-wheel-drive car.

'But I have to say that eventually when you fully understood the intricacies of the transmission and everything like the turbo lag then without question it was one of the most satisfying cars to drive. You just got an incredible amount of satisfaction out of being able to master it and get the best out of it. I didn't get the best out of it in '84 to be honest, towards the end of '84, the first season I did, but it was '85 when I really started to understand the car and what you could actually do with it. Personal satisfaction was just the best of anything that I've ever done.'

As a renowned team principal in today's world championship, as well as the constructor

RIGHT Maturing as a driver and as a team principal, Wilson's appearances on the world championship stage led to full-time drives with Austin-Rover and Ford, then to running Ford's WRC programme to claim drivers' and manufacturers' titles in the modern era. *(McKlein)*

of countless customer Ford Focus and Fiesta
rally cars that are in the hands of drivers all
over the globe, would Wilson consider offering
something as difficult to master today, if it gave
such a leap in performance over the opposition?

'I wouldn't say it was more demanding,' he
said. 'You know even the simple things, on the
Quattro at least, you had power steering so a
lot of things were easier. Where it was more
difficult was because to be able to extract the
best out of them it was trying to understand
the technique.

'A MkII Escort, you got in it and you knew
what it did, it did exactly what it said on the tin:
it went sideways and you didn't lose a lot of
speed. But the Quattro was just a completely
different animal in terms of it wasn't anything
like as forgiving, you had to work at the
technique, should we say, more than you did
with the two-wheel-drive car.'

Another British stalwart who got behind the
wheel of Audi's supercar was Andy Dawson, a
larger-than-life character who once cheerfully
drove a Datsun on which a curious symbol
appeared next to his name on the front wing
– a 'w' next to a painted anchor. This sort of
ebullience did not appear to be a natural fit with
the doughty Germanic character of the Quattro,
but Dawson found a way to bend it to his will.

'The Quattro was an animal that you had to
take by the scruff of the neck or let it do its own
thing,' he said.

'Michèle I think just let it do its own thing,
she found a way to work with the car and what
it wanted to do. Hannu, I think, was a bit 50-50,
in that he knew when and how to kick its ass
and make it do what he wanted it to do.'

Behind Dawson's warm good cheer lies a
technically brilliant mind and a fastidious team
management style, which suited taking the
Audis out for long-haul events around the world
such as the epic Hong Kong-Beijing, which his
cars won two years running. In 1985 the lead
car was driven by Mikkola, and Dawson was

amused by the Finn's approach to these cars given his long-standing experience.

'I remember saying to Hannu: "Do you want any changes made to the setup when we stop?" and he said: "I will drive it the way it is. They are all the same." It was a culture shock to me. I tried to race it to start with, that didn't work. I tried to sling it about and finally I was quicker than Hannu on one stage – but at that point I said: "That'll do!"'

Another driver who quickly found confidence in the Quattro was Sarel van der Merwe, celebrated in his native South Africa as 'Supervan'. As team leader on Audi's South African programme, he had the luxury of the type of gravel stages and wide-open savannah for which the big car's handling was best suited – and he made good use of the advantage.

'It was different but you knew you were driving a very potent car and it was a lot easier to win against the current competition initially before the other four-wheel-drive cars came along,' he remembered.

'You could actually, in a rally, experiment with different styles. You could try something on one stage and try something on another stage – all that sort of thing. So it was totally different but it was very exciting, really, and a great privilege to be in that car at that particular point in time. It wasn't that difficult to bring championships home, really.'

The only other driver to compete with van der Merwe for outright dominance in national competition was John Buffum, who was already by far the most experienced rally driver in his native North America. Buffum had left the army

ABOVE Sarel van der Merwe's lifelong association with Audi peaked with his domination of South African rallying. (Allan Durham collection)

and come to Europe in the late 1960s, where he discovered his pace and ability in the sport, and ultimately became a regular in Triumph TR7s on both sides of the Atlantic.

'I stopped Triumph in 1980 and in 1981 I really didn't actually have anything to do,' he said.

'Peugeot USA called me and said would I drive their 505 and 504, but by spring I had heard about the Quattro so I sort of stuck my nose in on the Porsche-Audi USA boss and said: "Hey, do you have any idea of bringing these cars over here?"

'He said yes, they had got the two-wheel-drive Audis that had been used by the works on the world championship in 1980, so I did six rallies with those. Luckily at the end of 1981 or beginning of 1982 he then decided to take the plunge and said: "Let's get the Quattro."'

BELOW LEFT John Buffum (centre) was the master of all he surveyed in North America, and proved himself a winner in Europe as well. (Fred Gallagher collection)

BELOW Buffum returned to Europe in 1983 as a privateer, shipping his American car over to the 1983 RAC Rally on his own budget. (McKlein)

'I got the car and I did the first rally in April, and while everyone talks about the quattro and the four-wheel drive it's also important to remember that with the turbo we had much more power than anyone else had. We had 300 or 320 horsepower in the 1982 car, and the Mazdas had under 300 horsepower, so not only did we have that traction advantage but also considerably more power available.'

Rod Millen's Mazda RX-7 was to become a notable rival, which in turn helped elevate the profile of rallying in the USA a hair or two higher than it might have been. Buffum's learning curve therefore had to be scaled in fairly short order at his first event, in which he had to pull back a deficit to the Mazda until he had got the hang of the car.

'The biggest thing I had to adapt to was not over-braking,' he said. 'So, in a two-wheel drive car, you go into the corner, turn into the corner and stab the brakes or apply some brake and because you have the brakes set up more on the rear this will start the rear of the car out and you can then play on the gas and the brakes to pull yourself round the corner, let's call it.

'I was doing that in the Quattro and it really didn't need to be balanced quite as much: you'd drive in, turn the wheel and drive out! So I would go in and brake as though I wanted

BELOW Jari-Matti Latvala drives today's WRC events for Toyota and is a beloved star of the series – but he also has a pair of Quattros to enjoy in his free time. *(Toyota Gazoo Racing World Rally Team)*

to get the rear of the car out, but I would slow from 60 mph to 30 mph and I didn't really need to – I could have got around the corner at 40 mph and then accelerated... But by the end of that first rally I was able to say "ah okay, this is what's happening" and I was able to get with the programme after that.'

For an enthusiastic gentleman driver, the challenges of the Quattro's behaviour could be particularly daunting. Greek rally ace 'Jigger' was a cavalier at the wheel, used to being able to throw his cars around and hold them on the throttle. He very soon discovered that this was not the Audi way of doing things.

'As a car it was difficult to drive, terribly difficult, for some simple reasons: by opening the hood you can see the motor is lengthways not transverse so it was loaded on the front, it was a strange balance and understeering like mad,' he said.

'It doesn't have a centre differential and so it doesn't have a handbrake. Later cars had a handbrake but the Quattro couldn't be drifted round a tight turn. It made life very hard on asphalt stages. We had to go back and forth to get round a tight turn, and we joked about it calling it a 'Comaneci' because you had to be flexible like a gymnast.

'The turbo lag was enormous. Terrific gaps

and you're waiting, literally, it feels like a normal car for one or two seconds maybe, then suddenly you're being pushed in the bucket seat. On the other hand, you lift off the gas and you're terrified because it kept pressurising, back pressure, the driver was braking but the car wanted to keep going fast.'

Changing times

The Audi Quattro is often cited as the foundation of modern rallying, which has been the province of turbocharged four-wheel-drive machinery through the eras since the 1980s, from the Lancia Delta Integrale to the Subaru Impreza and today's Hyundais, Citroëns, Toyotas and Fords. So is there any comparison between the cars that started the revolution and its descendants today?

One man knows: Jari-Matti Latvala. With 18 World Rally Championship wins to his name and a place at the forefront of the modern sport, he is proof positive that while the nature of the events has changed from gruelling treks to daily loops of timed stages, the spirit of rallying remains the same.

When he is not competing in a professional capacity he is most often to be found in his workshops restoring and preparing historic cars which give him the chance to get a flavour of the sport as it always was – including two Audi

Quattros. For him, the chance to get out there and drive the old Audis has been one of the biggest perks of his professional success, but he remains clear-eyed about their place next to modern machinery.

'I think that the rally has taken very good steps forward in recent years with the way that the cars have developed,' he said.

'They are fast like a Group B but things like the suspension are completely different and so on, but also the cars are a lot, lot, lot safer than they were in the eighties. You had the Kevlar bodies, the very lightweight roll cages and the fuel tanks were very close to the engine and not in a safe place.

'Audi brought the revolution, and when they brought the four-wheel drive that changed the sport forever. And I think that when Audi did the steps and the technology that they did at the time, they were big steps and you still see that today. The differentials and the turbos are now many steps on, but for sure that is the car that started it.'

Latvala's team principal for many years was Malcolm Wilson, the man who spotted the Finn's talent and who shares his views on the Quattro's place in history. 'I think the only big thing that you can derive today is that they were the people that brought four-wheel drive to rallying,' he said.

'That is the one single thing that, you know,

ABOVE Latvala travels back in time whenever his commitments allow, taking in classic Finnish stages to appreciate some of the sport's greatest heritage. *(Kaj Lindberg)*

BELOW The Ford
Escort RS1700T was
a sublime drivers' car,
but once the Quattro
appeared, Ford
abandoned the project
in favour of four-wheel
drive. (Author)

BOTTOM The Ford
RS200 resulted
from that decision:
a bespoke Group B
machine developed
with Formula 1
technology – rendering
the production-based
Quattro obsolete.
(Author)

there was a lot of doubt about at the time.
When it was announced that Audi was going to
rally a four-wheel-drive car a lot of people said
it would never work and what have you. But I
can go back to my Ford days when we were
doing the RS1700T and all the testing with a
transaxle, great balance in the car, great weight
distribution and then of course for a point we
still felt quite comfortable that was going to be
quite a competitive package but to be honest
with you it very quickly became clear that two-
wheel drive was not going to have any possible
success in the future.

'Ford then made the decision that to be
competitive you're going to have to have four-
wheel drive… I did the first event in the RS200
as well, the Lindisfarne, which we won in '85.

'Once you got onto a full Group B car with
four-wheel drive with the technology that was
evolving it was very evident that the Quattro
would not have a long shelf life – in its current
form, should we say… it became clear once I

started to drive the RS200, and at that time I
was driving rallies in the Quattro and testing the
RS200, and immediately you could see where
the advantages were of cars that were designed
purely for the job.'

The co-driver's view

All too often the co-drivers are overlooked in
the history of rallying. We all draw breath
at the sight of Mouton leaping through the air,
Röhrl dancing on the pedals and Blomqvist's
cornering geometry but there is much more to
the sport than those sort of heroics. There is
another equally important role being carried out.

'I think it's very important for a rally driver
and a navigator to get to know each other
well and also to know exactly what he's talking
about,' said Sarel van der Merwe. 'You know, if
he describes an intersection or something you
must be able to see the picture in your mind.'

Throughout his Audi career, and many more
seasons besides, 'Supervan' was partnered
with Franz Boschoff, who guided their car
with assurance… well, almost all the time. In
1984 'Supervan' was enjoying a prolific period
in his career, winning the Daytona 24 Hours
sports car race in America, taking part in the Le
Mans 24 Hours in a Porsche 956 and heading
towards another South African title with Audi.
Audi Sport also invited him to join the factory
team on the 1984 Portugal Rally – which
resulted in a rather early exit.

'We went and I was in Portugal for three
weeks preparing for the rally and then on one of
the stages, Franz turns over about two pages
and as luck would have it the instruction was
almost the same. The page that we should
have been on said "crest, 90 left" and the one
that he turned to said "crest-flat".

'So I went flying and was looking out of the
window where down below us the road went
left and unfortunately that was the end of our
Portuguese rally. But we ran quite competitively
and I was having quite a good dice with Stig at
that time. It was nice to be part of the official
rally team, because being part of the official rally
team in Europe and part of the official rally team
in South Africa were two different things.'

One partnership that was less long-standing
but achieved great things was that of American

driver John Buffum and Northern Irish co-driver Fred Gallagher. The intensely focused Buffum and easy-going Gallagher had to work fast to establish some ground rules in the cockpit, however.

'I've always enjoyed the co-driver aspect and I remember somewhere along the way I was thinking about something that I wasn't sure if we'd checked,' Buffum chuckled. 'So I asked and Fred turned and looked at me and he said: "I won't ask for your steering wheel; don't you ask for my paperwork!"'

Gallagher also had fond memories of his three events in an Audi with Buffum in 1984, which brought victories in the North American series, in Cyprus on the FIA European Rally Championship and then a career-best fifth place in a world championship event: the Acropolis Rally.

'John was a very capable driver and probably an intelligence level above most of the opposition,' Gallagher said.

'I strongly believe that good drivers know how to drive and I never really reined anyone

ABOVE A great example of the teamwork between driver and co-driver can be seen in the successes of John Buffum and Fred Gallagher. *(Fred Gallagher collection)*

BELOW Sarel van der Merwe and Franz Boschoff joined the Audi Sport team once in 1984 – a memorable experience in many ways for the South African stars. *(McKlein)*

back – I never tried to slow anybody down. If they need to be reined back either you're scared and in the wrong job or they're too quick and in the wrong job! You're working, you strap yourself in tight, you sit down in the seat and your job's to read your notes, it's not to look out of the window.'

The first and arguably most valuable part of the job was making those notes in the first place. This is what filled far more of a co-driver's calendar than the competitive days, as Gallagher explained:

'Apart from the Safari, you would want to ideally go out on an event four weeks in advance of starting competitively,' he said.

'Some events were restricted – Sweden and Finland were restricted, but other events like the Acropolis were completely free. Absolutely it was a full-time job.'

Recce trips by their very nature provide some of the best examples of co-driver anecdotes, of a kind in which Gallagher excels. One Audi-related incident that he recalled came on the fateful 1985 Ivory Coast event from which Michèle Mouton's Audi was eventually withdrawn. By the sounds of it, that was hardly the worst moment of the event.

'I was with Juha [Kankkunen] and Björn Waldegård and Michèle and all three crews were going around together,' Gallagher recounted.

'One would set off from control and the other would wait a minute or two and go. We set off at rally speed, we were in rally cars although it was a recce, and I remember coming round the corner and there was an Audi bonnet in the road, then we got further round the corner and there was an Audi sitting without any doors, basically no front, steam coming out of it...

'Bizarrely she'd come round the corner and there was a railway crossing and the train was coming. She hit the train between the wheels and bounced back and the train driver tried to stop but it took him about a mile to stop down the road and then of course all the passengers came running back. I've got some nice pictures of that somewhere – one of those things that should be famous but isn't!

'We had about 300km (186 miles) to get back to Yamoussoukro – I say "we", but not me, because I'm not a mechanic. Basically between Björn and Juha and Arne Hertz, who was in with Michèle, they cobbled the car together. It didn't have any doors or anything!

'Kankkunen drove the Audi, Björn went ahead and made pace notes for all of us and I drove the other Celica Twin-Cam Turbo with Michèle Mouton as my passenger – something that she doesn't remember a thing about!'

The opportunity to join John Buffum's team in 1984 also brought examples of the

RIGHT Fred Gallagher (left) and Toyota team-mates Kankkunen, Waldegård and Thorzelius came to Michèle Mouton's aid in the Ivory Coast after a dramatic moment on recce. (McKlein)

willingness for rival teams and crews to chip in and help one another out. Indeed, the very fact that he was in the car at all was proof of that.

'All the top people had season-long contracts,' Gallagher said. 'In '84, for example, which was my first year with Toyota, they took a fairly liberal view about me doing it. Not that they would have been quite so relaxed if I had been in a works car, of course, but this was a totally Buffum programme – if he hadn't driven it nobody else was going to drive it. He arranged the sponsorship, he did the deal with Sutton, he got Graham Rood as team manager. Graham's a very capable man: a doctor of sonic booms who worked at Farnborough but came along as team manager both on Cyprus and Acropolis when we were there.'

Buffum's car in North America was sponsored by tyre giant BF Goodrich and this proved to be the key in getting a string of overseas appearances together. 'BF Goodrich wanted to sell tyres in Europe so in '84 they and I made a deal where, okay, give me some money and I'll go over and do five events in Europe, so they were happy – so it was a BF Goodrich-oriented thing,' Buffum said.

'I went and got a price from Schmidt and Sutton to do the five rallies with them. And Schmidt, being German, was always a little bit more so I went with Sutton. Sutton prepared their car, it was their British car or whatever, WVN 44, that was the car I used.'

The BF Goodrich budget didn't quite cover all the costs, however – and here's where that good old spirit of rallying came into play once again.

'On the Acropolis we were only able to recce the stages for the first two days. But Fred borrowed Vatanen's notes for the Peloponnese and they worked very well for us.'

Despite being able to copy the homework of Ari Vatanen's co-driver, Terry Harryman, Gallagher's presence in the car on the stages that they had not recce'd also paid huge dividends by virtue of his skill, as Buffum was keen to report.

'I remember going down a stage and the note was something like "Fast right through junction" but when we got there it was a Y junction and I said: "Well, which way?"

And immediately, not missing a beat, Fred called out "Stay left" because he had kept the route book open under his notes and was able to follow along where he was while he was reading the notes and that impressed me so much. If we had our top 20 of rally drivers, he is well inside the top 20 of co-drivers.'

ABOVE With BF Goodrich backing and David Sutton's team behind them, Buffum and Gallagher's adventures on the 1984 Acropolis resulted in the American's best-ever WRC result. *(McKlein)*

Chapter Seven

The owner's view

The classic car world in general, and the classic motor sport world in particular, represents a marketplace for investment like few others. For more than a decade, the relentless rise in values has given owners a higher return on investment than gold, wine or art – providing that you have the right car, that is. A genuine factory-built Audi Quattro has the provenance and scarcity to be one of the most sought-after cars of the 1980s but there are many ways to experience the joys of driving one of these remarkable rally cars, although they all demand a degree of passion and commitment.

OPPOSITE For fans around the world, the opportunity exists to see the great stars and cars of the past reunited at big historic events. Here Walter Röhrl takes owner Wolf-Dieter Ihle for a spin in his old Sport quattro S1 at the Eifel Rallye Festival. *(Lawrence Clift)*

ABOVE The value of any historic car is in its provenance, which can be hard to trace with rally cars. For auction houses such as Bonhams, identifying the wood from the trees is important in ensuring the confidence of bidders. *(Bonhams)*

How to buy a Quattro

A favourite topic of conversation is to pick cars for your dream garage, and for many people an Audi Quattro rally car will be near the top of the list. Yet relatively few collectors today have got one of these iconic cars sitting at home – so how would a potential owner go about finding one?

Bonhams is one of the leading auction houses for historic racing cars and the consignments for its sales, particularly those at major events like Goodwood in the UK, draw a mouth-watering array of exotica. This is where the dream of owning a unique, historic racing car gains the spice of competitive bidding to win headlines around the world – and John Polson has been responsible for many of the choicest consignments in recent years.

'Audi Quattros very rarely come up,' he said. 'Audi's hung on to a lot of them but they're iconic rally cars, Group B cars and the four-wheel-drive pioneers, so undoubtedly they are highly sought-after. If you think of any cars of that era you've got the Golf GTi road car and the Audi Quattro rally car right up there as the most iconic of their time. We'd like to see more of them.'

An alternative is to go to a specialist in the field to help track down a car and make a private sale. Surrey-based Mark Donaldson has an intimate knowledge of the 1980s rally scene, thanks in no small part to being raised around Group B cars that his father Ian competed in. He has often made eager buyers' dreams come true, but acknowledges that rally cars, and in particular Quattros, can be tricky to source.

'Cars with a more juicy history will put you into a really difficult sector where you've got a not-necessarily committed seller and a nervous buyer and so you might have to go off-piste to get a sale,' he said. 'When you put something on the market and it sells, so it's been taken off the market, then that really makes potential buyers then sit up and take note of where and when the next opportunity to buy may come from, so very often you will see that the next car to come along sells for a much higher sum.'

In rural Somerset lies a Mecca for Quattro connoisseurs: AM Cars, run with the encyclopaedic knowledge of Adam Marsden. Whether it is a Quattro for road or rally use, he and his team can source, restore, service and give guidance to long-standing owners or excited first-timers. One of the big problems with any rally car, he explained, was with the provenance – and Audi was no different to any other manufacturer in that respect.

'It's very difficult because the factory used to chop and change number plates. I remember a case, and there are several cases, where there is more than one example of the same car with the same identity. It wasn't done deliberately, certainly not at the time, but when you look at a

BELOW More value is placed on cars that can headline major public events as the stars of the show. An Audi will tick every owner's box on this front. *(Lawrence Clift)*

rally workshop at the time, how much work was going on with the cars, how many events they were doing? There was a degree of finishing a car off for an event, screwing on the number plates and going off to compete.'

So what is the value of an Audi Quattro rally car as the 40th anniversary of its career comes in to view on the horizon? Mark Donaldson believes that if the paperwork is in order, the scarcity of Quattros makes them among the most valuable rally cars in the world.

'With Quattro values, it's very, very hard with all the derivatives – Group 4, Group B A1/A2, the Sport and S1 E2 – to give a general price for a "rally Quattro",' he said.

'It's all theoretical because sales of genuine cars are so rare. A real Group 4 car is probably going to be 300,000–500,000 Euros [£260,000–£430,000] and they will be the most popular and user-friendly. An A1 will probably be tougher to sell because people will either want the original Group 4 or, in the long-wheelbase cars, the A2 as that was the big butch one.

'I would say that the A2 is the right car for people like me, it's so big and it won both of the drivers' world championships and a manufacturers' championship so if a good, genuine one presents itself that's easily between half a million and 750,000 Euros [£430,000–£650,000].'

In total, Matter built 61 long-wheelbase cars, given identities beginning with the 'R' prefix, from the first prototype R1 through to the Group 4 era and into Group B ending in 1984 with R61. A further 22 Audi Sport quattros were built in 1984, which carried RS prefixes from RS01 to RS22. A further 20 evolution cars, the bewinged Audi Sport quattro S1, were built in 1985 carrying the numbers RE01–RE20.

Out of these cars, Audi has retained a phenomenal number – and is constantly on the lookout for opportunities to buy back more of the cars to this day. Andy Dawson is the keeper of R61, the 1984 Argentine Rally winner and twice winner of the Hong Kong–Beijing marathon, and he recently declined an offer to sell it back to the firm that built it.

'Ingolstadt bought the Sutton collection off the Americans who had it. Everything,' said Quattro expert Adam Marsden. 'All of the old cars like 44 CMN and MVV 44Y are at Ingolstadt. They had LYV 4X at the new dealership in Hammersmith for a launch and one of the big cheeses from

ABOVE Audi let very few of its cars into private hands in period, and has sought to buy back many of those in private hands. Seeing them in public is a rare privilege. *(McKlein/Slowly Sideways)*

ABOVE Audi UK is custodian of the Sport quattro S1 driven by Röhrl and Mills on the 1985 RAC Rally with PDK transmission. After being rebuilt it first went to Austrian rallycross star Herbert Breiteneder and endured a long, hard life before restoration.

Ingolstadt was there and said words to the effect of "what's this doing here – get it gone!" and nobody's seen that one since it went onto a truck heading back to Ingolstadt.'

Audi remains fiercely protective of its cars, just as it was in period. This helps to add to the mystique of the Quattro and the few cars that exist in private hands. It also does wonders for their value in today's marketplace.

'Genuine short wheelbase quattros are in short supply,' Mark Donaldson confirmed. 'I believe there are five of the original Sport quattro cars representative of how they were in period, ready to go on the button, of which three are in private hands. Audi's got most of them, there's one on the continent, one in Ireland and the Pikes Peak 1985 winner, which is still in the USA. I don't see anything less than a million Euros [£863,000] for one of those. There really isn't an upper limit on one of those cars.

'Then you get to the final S1 E2 and they appeared in only five world championship rallies… so that really is a rarity, and the pinnacle as a collector. Theoretically you won't see change from a million Euros, an owner would want 1.5 [£1.3 million] and to be honest when you show buyers that footage of the 1,000 Lakes when they are wheelie-ing under power that is incredible and that sort of "bullying factor" can really make the difference.'

Building a Quattro

Without doubt, the most popular route to ownership today is through building a replica. With the FIA content to sanction replica Quattros provided that they meet the same homologation criteria as the cars built in Ingolstadt 40 years ago, tired old road cars have been born anew as authentic working rally cars that can cope with charging through rally stages at a suitable pace.

Adam Marsden was one of the pioneers of the movement, and when David Sutton

LEFT This is a replica of the same S1 wearing Breiteneder's livery. Audi Tradition and the Breiteneder family have endorsed the high calibre of workmanship – but it is in no way to be considered the real thing. *(Author)*

closed down his celebrated business it was Marsden who bought all of the spare parts, toolings, moulds and patterns needed to carry on constructing and servicing works-spec cars long into the future at AM Quattro.

His first build was a replica of the car in which Hannu Mikkola gave the Quattro its FIA World Rally Championship debut on the 1981 Monte Carlo Rally. Everything about the car is exactly as it was on that fateful week in the Alpes Maritimes when the Quattro changed the shape of the sport forever – to the point where even Mikkola himself felt right at home in the car.

'In those days, back in the nineties, there was no Internet so there was a lot of scavenging and old photos, and Sutton's gave us LYV 4X to go over and measure and do what we needed,' he said.

'I'd have said that it was probably the first real "copy car" that was built in this country. It was also the first one to have an FIA passport because they just didn't have a clue where to start. But it started a bit of a movement off – we took it to Chatsworth and then Nick Barrington was probably the next one to build something close. He and I both did this wonderful event together on the French–Swiss borders and we could put them on studded tyres and all that

ABOVE IT executive Nick Barrington was able to call upon the expertise of David Sutton's rally team to ensure that his replica Quattro was as close to the original as possible. *(Author)*

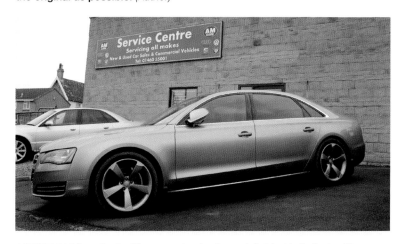

ABOVE AM Cars looks like a regular Audi specialist but is in fact a Mecca for Quattro owners, restorers and enthusiasts. *(Author)*

BELOW Adam Marsden built the first authentic replica Quattro rally car with this nut-and-bolt recreation of Hannu Mikkola's 1981 Monte Carlo Rally entry.

BELOW Marsden's handiwork fooled Hannu Mikkola and Arne Hertz who were amazed at the attention to detail with blue seatbelts, bespoke door bags and an original toolkit completing the effect. *(Adam Marsden collection)*

RIGHT To showcase
AM Cars' abilities,
Marsden built 'the
beast' – namely a long
wheelbase Quattro A1
fitted with the Sport
quattro's 20-valve
engine, the car that
Stig Blomqvist wished
he could have had in
period. *(Author)*

– there are some very pleasant events to do in these cars.'

Since then, AM Quattro has either built or been involved in the build of a multitude of other cars that have become regular crowd pleasers. For Adam Marsden, this has included a rolling advertisement for what his firm can do in the form of an Audi Quattro A1 – arguably the rarest of all the sub-types – which has been fitted with a full 420 bhp 20-valve engine from a Sport quattro.

'Stig Blomqvist has always said that the Sport quattro was a bad idea, and that in his mind the ultimate would have been the 20-valve engine in the long-wheelbase car,' Marsden said.

'Well, if it's good enough for Stig then it's good enough for me – so I built it. And it's a beast. It's a bit scary sometimes I don't mind saying but it really does shift and people love seeing it out there. Stig thought it went really

well at Whiscombe Park when he drove it on the RAC thing. It's a proper '83 car, exactly smack-on... apart from the "Stig" engine swap!'

Many of the photos in this book are of the latest and final car that Marsden is building for his personal fleet – an Audi Quattro A2. This car, using the original moulds used in period, will be the most authentic replica Group B car that Adam Marsden has built – and he is very excited about the prospect.

'I can't tell you what the livery will be. I want that to be a surprise when we first roll the car out at its first event. But I shan't be building any more for myself – at the moment I've got the Group 4, the A1 and the Group A 200 quattro as they were on the 1987 Monte Carlo Rally. The A2 completes the set for me,' he said.

One newly minted Quattro owner looking forward to many years of Quattro action is Bob 'Log' Dennis – a former British Tarmac rally champion. For him, owning a Quattro is the realisation of a dream that goes back to the halcyon days of the RAC Rally, when the likes of Mikkola and Blomqvist blasted through forests near Dennis's home.

'I was a forestry lad, I worked in the forest, so I naturally saw them non-stop coming through and the Audis were just groundbreaking,' he said. 'I just thought that, as a kid without a coin to scratch my backside with, I just thought, "one day..."'

Dennis built up a successful lumber business and this helped to fund an amateur rally career, winning his first championship in 2002. By 2006 he and co-driver Ronnie Rufford won the prestigious National Tarmac Championship in

BELOW Completing
Adam Marsden's
personal collection
will be this replica
Audi Quattro A2. He
is planning to reveal
it in much-loved livery
wearing details like
the original car's rally
plates. *(Author)*

their Subaru but recuperation from a major back operation drew a line under Dennis's rally career at that point.

The bug never left him, however, and when a friend from the rally world showed him the Datsun 240 Z that he had just restored, the idea of historic rallying seemed too good to miss. 'I looked at a Chevette and stuff like that but I just thought, no, if I'm going to do that it's got to be a Quattro,' he said.

Dennis bought the first and only rally-prepared Quattro that he discovered for sale – and then immediately stripped it down to a bare shell. If he was going to live his dream of sampling a little of what his heroes had done, then he wanted his car to be as close as possible to theirs.

'I couldn't find an ex-works rally car unless you're talking six figures and so I settled on something that I could build right back to the correct specification,' he said.

'I dropped on this one, but this was rough so it was a case of stripping it to 1,000 bits and building it back right and take my time to build it. All the parts are hand-made, all hand-folded and so on. The cage all stayed in, that's homologated, but all the suspension and the diff underneath is all brand new.

'I've had the correct templates and had the parts made and pressed in by hand. I've got 1,450 pictures on my phone of Quattro components and this is what you have to work with. I work off pictures, the colours are all perfect. It's blooming hard when you're working off that! I've wanted to do it right, this car's become like a baby to me. It's got new shafts for the transmission, these are the refurbed original driveshafts, the brakes are original but all refurbed.

'I'm not a mechanic – I'm a timber-feller, I'm a woodman – but you can work it out. I've had so many parts sent away to make brand new and when it's done it will be beautiful. Something to be proud of, anyway. I've had to do quite a bit.'

LEFT If you've ever wondered what holds a Quattro together, Bob Dennis can show you. Every nut and bolt removed from his Quattro is ready to be reinstalled. *(Author)*

BELOW Nick Barrington's car was built for his enjoyment and right-hand drive allows him to feel more at home behind the wheel. That aside, you need to look hard to find any difference to the real McCoy. *(Author)*

Another enthusiastic owner is Nick Barrington, a former IT executive who spent several years working with the support of members of the David Sutton team to create his own picture-perfect replica of LYV 4X, the celebrated British championship car that stars on the cover of this book.

'I started mine in 2005 and I finished the build in 2013, first on the road in May, and we had a few teething problems and took it to Race Retro the following year,' he said.

'When we got there, Adam [Marsden] said:

"It's a beautiful job but why didn't you make it left-hand drive?"

'The thing is for me that I'm familiar with driving on the right, and pushing a car hard through a stage I'd rather be sitting on the right because it's more second nature. And I'm not trying to fool anyone that this is an original car so I therefore don't need to put the wheel in the same place that it had been as an original car.'

Although making no pretence that his car is the genuine article, Barrington made no concession to the authenticity of its construction in the eight-year build process. In doing so he got himself in and under almost every genuine car that he could find; an odyssey that has taken him into the thick of the ongoing fascination with works cars among Quattro cognoscenti.

'There are all sorts of little details that you don't find in the homologation papers and you don't necessarily pick up in the car when you are just looking at one that is fully assembled,' he said.

'Did they have double-skinned suspension turrets? Did they have a double-skinned front bulkhead? I don't know! Some of the cars that I've seen around, originals, appear to have been built from Coupé quattro shells I think because there is no evidence of the opening for the battery box being plated over. Others are like mine, and like the original 4X, must have been originally a turbo shell because it did have the plated battery box in it.'

Quattros in the wild

'The thing with competition cars is generally their value is very much connected to what you can do with them,' said Bonhams' expert, John Polson.

'If you can do the Monte Carlo Historique, the Le Mans Classic or Goodwood Revival then that has a very positive impact on their value. As we saw with the Group 1 touring cars, once there was a race for them at the Goodwood Members' Meeting, their value went stratospheric.'

The rally cars of the sport's most electrifying era were generally viewed as problem children by the sport's authorities and were overlooked until owners and the public started to take matters into their own hands. 'There's a lot of owners who want somewhere to go and run their cars, a lot are demonstrations and some of the drivers want to run their cars in anger,' said Allan Durham.

'They used to send them out at intervals among the classes actually competing, but that all got rather competitive as well, so the FIA had to put a stop to it! They've got to run in convoy these days, so now there's more specialist events. Goodwood could well develop its rally area at the Festival of Speed but it's a bit far out of the way of the main event for a lot of owners – if you've got a lovely historic rally car you want to feel like part of the main event.'

Race Retro has become a focal point of the calendar for owners and enthusiasts of historic rally cars, being held each February in the National Agriculture Centre at Stoneleigh. The owners' group Rallying With Group B musters a decent selection of cars each year to run through roughly 50 stage miles (80km)in the course of the weekend, and it provides a welcome start to the social calendar for all enthusiasts of the type.

'We knew that a lot of people wanted to see the cars, and that a lot of owners were out there with perfectly well-maintained, original cars that just had no outlet for them,' said Tim Foster, head of the Rallying With Group B organisation.

'Race Retro means that people can come and see them doing something representative, see the owners having fun with them, and even if it's not a full rally we're always trying to keep the stages fresh so that people enjoy driving

them and to make sure that the cars are seen and enjoyed.'

For most owners, six or seven weekends of the year are spent taking in events across Europe. 'Goodwood, Belgium, Germany, France, two in Italy and the Spanish one,' said Adam Marsden of his 2019 schedule for the Group 4 and Group B Quattros that he has built.

'Reinhard Klein wants us to do Catalunya, and he seems to be growing that one quite nicely. He and (former Austin Rover team principal) John Davenport have developed the

ABOVE Replicas run alongside genuine examples on the major events – although the most historic cars tend to stay off the gravel these days. *(McKlein/Slowly Sideways)*

BELOW Wearing full Ivory Coast accessories such as the spotlights and 'roo bar, this Sport quattro is pure eye candy for rally fans of all ages. *(McKlein/Slowly Sideways)*

ABOVE If you have a car or not, some accessories are always welcome to see. Adam Marsden sparked a craze for creating replica service barges with this Volkswagen LT. *(Author)*

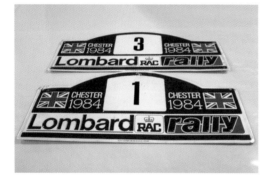

RIGHT Also in Adam Marsden's collection are these RAC Rally plates – Stig Blomqvist's number 1 never having been used after his car was withdrawn. *(Author)*

RIGHT Team uniforms were not as integral to team identities as they are now, but Audi's original rally jackets are now worth hundreds in any currency. *(Author)*

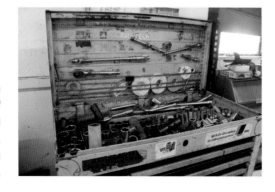

RIGHT Allan Durham's tool box saw years of hard service around Quattros in Africa, Europe and China through the 1980s.

Eifel Rally Legends into a good one. The one in Vosges is really becoming good now… it does cost a bit of money to do but the good events are really well put together and the response of people when they see the cars makes it all worthwhile.'

For specialist dealer, Mark Donaldson, these events offer an opportunity to savour. 'The two most prominent events are Rally Legend in Italy and the Eifel Classic in Germany,' he said.

'There are a lot of smaller events but none has yet got the perfect combination of the cars being the centrepiece of that event. A lot of owners want to feel that their cars are what people have come to see and there isn't that specific event yet.'

When it comes to finding the ideal way to present the cars, Donaldson has a particular role model in mind. 'Last year's Le Mans Classic was actually up by about 15,000 on attendance – which is great news for the whole sport when the number of competition licence holders has fallen and spectators at club events are a rare phenomenon indeed.

'It's bloody awesome that the Le Mans Classic has rebuffed that and so I think there's a lesson there that if there's an event to be done of that scale it should be biannual. it should be all eras not just Group B, in order to put a good spectator show on. You need a central base to highlight the cars, a static display area... what I'd do is a rolling show, in the UK and Europe. I'd try to bring in a bit of an experience of the era like Goodwood has done with the Revival. There are some great possibilities, I believe.'

BELOW This note was scribbled in marker pen after Durham built a new set of wishbones in 1984. *(Author)*

For the owners of original factory-built cars, their increasing value is a factor in deciding which events to do. It will be rare to see a genuine works car out on a gravel rally stage in the modern era, for example, although a demonstration on paved roads will bring more out. It's all about protecting the investment – as Allan Durham knows.

'There will always be a collector with an open chequebook for a genuine Audi Sport car so it is silly to wrap it round a tree or have the worst-case scenario of it catching fire,' he said.

'That very nearly happened to this car [IN-NX 47] when I put it off up on the Isle of Mull. I went off on a very slippy section and went backwards down this big drop and it still had its old bag tank in and it was leaking around the nose.

'We'd only previously filled up before going into that stage and fuel was leaking out of the cap into the boot and the battery's in the boot and, you know, it only needed one spark and it would have gone. And you don't think about them things until it happens and then you think: "Hold on – should we have taken the car through the forest like this?"'

Bonhams expert, John Polson, also believes that owners of cars that are in full period trim will always be at a disadvantage in historic

competition. 'If you look at the pre-war grand prix cars for example, if you were to put an Alfa or one of the Auto Unions or Mercedes out in one of those races it would struggle to stay with the ERAs, which never would have happened in period, but people have spent the last 80-odd years making the ERAs go faster.

'It's the same with a Group C Le Mans car, for example: if you've got a factory Rothmans Porsche 956, it's got to be exactly period spec to realise its value and you'll find someone with a far less competitive car in period that's been evolved to a much higher level of performance today.'

ABOVE The definition of pride in ownership: Adam Marsden's fleet gives him and historic rally fans across Europe enormous pleasure each year. *(Author)*

LEFT Allan Durham looks after this priceless ex-works and 555 Rally Team car and knows how easy it is to put these cars in jeopardy. *(Author)*

Celica Group A in ST165, ST185 and ST205 trim and a Corolla WRC. But sitting between them in the Latvala Motorsport Museum is a pair of Audi Quattros.

'I myself have the Audi Group 4 and the Audi Group B A2 Quattro,' he said. 'To me the A2 was the nicest car to drive. It is very stable and also the power… you do feel the turbo and the turbo lag but when you are prepared you can cope with that. When you get to the S1 you have a lot more power, about 600 horsepower, and everything was a lot more aggressive. That car, if you were not on top of it, it's controlling you and that's never good!'

Happy the man whose work is also his hobby – and with his living, breathing museum of landmark cars, Latvala both welcomes visitors and takes the cars out to sample something of the sport's history for himself.

'Basically how I keep them is I keep them in a driving condition that I can go out whenever I want to,' he said. 'They are not completely museum cars.

'My passion is to be able to drive whatever the car is, how difficult it is, always to be able to control the car. And if I think about the Audi, with the heavy front, it is understeering in the entry of the slow corners but how you avoid it is a small Scandinavian flick and the rest of it you sort out on the throttle.

'And actually the car is very stable on the fast corners, so really it's only the tight corners you have to work for the car. The car itself is like a tank – the suspension, the arms and everything, the car is very, very strong. The only thing is that with the engine and all that weight on the front, when you do the jumps there is the risk that you bend the chassis legs a bit.'

Latvala was driving with Volkswagen Motorsport when he decided to take the plunge into Quattro ownership. 'The first car was the Group 4 car, it was built in Italy and they had the original parts so they did the car over there,' he said.

'After that, for the second car the chassis was built in Poland and we assembled the engine and gearbox ourselves. It was a hard job, I can tell you, finding the parts. The Group 4 car came quite easily because I ordered the car, they built it for just a bit less than one year and then that car was ready. Then the Group B Quattro took two

ABOVE Jari-Matti Latvala had his Group 4 car built to exact period specifications, including the tricky Pierburg fuel injection.
(Kaj Lindberg)

BELOW After enjoying several historic rallies with the car, Latvala intends to place it in the museum that he has opened in order to preserve it for less strenuous work.
(Kaj Lindberg)

Homage from a hero

To fans of rallying in the modern era, Jari-Matti Latvala is one of the fastest and most admired men in the sport. He is, in the words of Malcolm Wilson, the only driver who could 'scare' nine-time world champion Sébastien Loeb with his pace, and his approachable manner has kept him firmly in the public's affection.

These days he competes and wins WRC rallies with the works Toyota team, but at home he has built up a small but exclusive stable of cars, representing the heritage of the teams for which he has driven.

In his years at Ford, Latvala built a period-specification Ford Escort RS1800 to throw around the forests at home. Today he is building four of Toyota's most celebrated rally cars – the

years because some very, very rare parts and special parts were not easy to find.

'A genuine aluminium engine block was already one challenge, and then the inlet manifold was one challenge, then I couldn't find transmissions so we actually had to produce new transmission in Finland. I got a guy who was able to do the work and all that took one year.'

For friends, family and fans in Finland it is a regular occurrence to see Latvala out in the forests taking part in historic events alongside other enthusiasts and owners – among them Anteiro Laine, the national champion in period with his original factory-built Quattro A2. In future, however, Latvala will be limiting his competitive outings to the Group B car and will keep the Group 4 car for personal enjoyment.

'Because it has a mechanical Pierburg fuel injection, actually we now have problems with the Group 4 car,' he said.

'If you don't drive with it there's a rubber seal inside and the rubber starts to get hard and doesn't work properly and there's a risk that you get engine failure because of that. So now I've decided that the Group 4 I won't use anymore, but the Group B car has electronic fuel injection, so that one I can use basically whenever I want to.'

As was the case in period, Finland's fast forest stages have proven to be the ideal environment in which to get a taste of what the sport was all about in the 1980s. Indeed, to much surprise, Latvala even prefers taking the Quattro out for a run to the light and nimble Ford Escort.

'The RS1800 has a beautiful sound when you are revving up to 10,000rpm and rear-drive is such good fun to drive but if I go very fast like on Finland-style special stages I enjoy it more with the Audi,' he said.

'The Audi is more stable in the high-speed places plus with the power steering it's a little bit easier to control the stages. If there is a stage with 120kph [75mph] average speed, I feel more comfortable in the Audi!

'When I'm in the car, in my opinion I need to be able to drive relaxed, I need to drive that I don't need to worry about being too careful about the big jumps and things like that. But for sure when you drive hard in a world rally car, you can't approach jumps in the same way. The car was made in the eighties, it doesn't have the same suspension travel, the weight

ABOVE Latvala's Audi outings will now be focused on enjoying his Group B Quattro A2, lovingly recreated in Finland and much better suited to regular hard running. *(Kaj Lindstrom)*

BELOW At home in his garage with the two rally Quattros, Jari-Matti has also restored a Quattro road car, Ford Escort RS1800 and four Toyotas. *(Helena Latvala)*

distribution and everything has been very pushed forward by comparison so you have to drive as in period.'

Although he is still very much enjoying life as a professional star of the World Rally Championship today, Latvala is looking forward to enjoying his collection for many years after the end of his career. Indeed, not only is he building his Toyota fleet but he is also adding more Audis to the museum.

'Something I wanted to mention is that I have the Group 4, the Group B and I have an Ur-Quattro road car. I have this one and we are hopefully finishing by next year an Audi Coupé Group A quattro,' he said. Despite having more than enough ability to master the mighty S1, he is unlikely to add one of the 600bhp cars to his fleet, however.

'I managed to drive three years ago with Wolf-Dieter Ihle, who owns an ex-Mouton S1. He let me test it in Rally Legend – and I tell you that it is an experience! It's amazing but it's so expensive and so rare that my target is not to go that way.'

Hidden treasures

Around the world, those owners who have managed to get their hands on genuine cars from the period hold an enormous slice of the rich history of rallying. In Finland, preparation expert Kari Mäkelä builds modern and historic cars for his customers on a regular basis – but the star of his workshop is IN-NL 67, build number R46, which was the first of the full Group B Quattro A2 models to have started a World Rally Championship event.

After crashing out on its debut on the 1983 Tour de Corse, the lightweight shell with its hand-operated clutch went on to be driven by Michèle Mouton in the 1,000 Lakes. Mikkola then returned to the cockpit to drive the car on the Ivory Coast Rally, with a heavier-duty gearbox and suspension, to claim second place on the rally and claim the FIA World Rally Championship for Drivers.

The car sat idle at Ingolstadt during 1984, but the following year it was sold to Cypriot star Dimi Mavropoulos, who duly won honours in national rallying and international rallycross events, wearing his celebrated black livery. When Marvopoulos retired the car, it ended up in the hands of a Finnish enthusiast who drove it in sprints and autotests until parking it in a barn – where it remained for 14 years.

Finally, in 2018, the car emerged from a ten-year restoration by its current owner, Kari Mäkelä. It is a car that he spared no expense in putting back to completely authentic period trim in the guise of its debut event in Corsica 35 years earlier, and which today stands as a shining testament to the Audi Sport team of the time – and to Mäkelä Auto Tuning today.

'The car is currently fitted with its original bodyshell, all its original mechanical parts, rare aluminium cylinder block, lightweight short gearbox, and its original and correct chassis (with its chassis stamp matching the original documentation on file),' Mäkelä said.

'The car's history has been well documented, with its history file including Audi Sport data sheets and documentation from the thorough restoration, including 1,500 detailed photographs throughout the ten-year process. It is fully prepped to compete in international historic events and races today, and as the only four-wheel-drive Group B historic cars allowed to participate in official FIA historic rallies, it will surely be welcomed by event organisers and fans alike.'

LEFT One of the most interesting histories of any Quattro rally car is that of IN-NX 47. Its first outing brought Walter Röhrl's historic victory on the 1984 Monte Carlo Rally.

ABOVE Audi Tradition has a genuine A2 wearing the colours of Röhrl's winning car – but in fact it is wearing the 555 Rally Team colours carried when driven by Andy Dawson in China. *(Audi AG)*

RIGHT IN-NX 47 is also believed to be the only rally Quattro to have won honours in circuit racing – here is Andy Dawson on his way to victory in Thundersaloons competition. *(Gary Walton)*

RIGHT New Zealand rally driver Malcolm Stewart bought one of the Quattro A2s from Audi Sport at the end of the 1984 event, painting it in the striking Enzed livery. *(McKlein)*

Audi Tradition in Ingolstadt holds so many of the original works cars in store that it is hard to know where to start in picking one car out. Only one of the Quattros appears at a time in the company museum, while a handful are maintained in full running order for media and public events around the world.

One of these cars carries the registration number IN-NX 47 and the livery of Walter Röhrl's victorious car from the 1984 Monte Carlo Rally – but in fact this one is slightly misleading. The real car actually resides more than 900 miles (1,450km) away in Lancashire, wearing the 555 Rally Team colours that it carried in Andy Dawson's hands in China. This car also has the honour of being the only works Audi Quattro to have won a circuit race, which was another highlight of its time in Dawson's hands.

'We had just got it back from rebuild and I wanted to give it a run,' Dawson beamed. 'The car was painted white and I entered it in the Thundersaloons race… stuck it on the front row and I was side-by-side with John Cleland for a lap and a half looking across and grinning at each other. He had that Vauxhall Commodore thing, the big Brock Holden basically from Bathurst, and then of course it started raining and with the four-wheel-drive "vrrrppp" I was off and away!'

On the other side of the world, in the Oamaru Auto Collection in New Zealand, resides IN-YD 29, which was a gravel-specification car and was first used on the 1984 Portugal Rally, driven by Stig Blomqvist who crashed heavily. Subsequently rebuilt, Blomqvist had better fortune with the car on the Acropolis

Rally, taking victory, before it was packed up and shipped off for the New Zealand Rally.

Hannu Mikkola finished third with the car, despite rolling it and catching fire. Local competitor Malcolm Stewart then bought the car from the team, retaining the New Zealand registration MB1440 that it was issued on arrival, and repainted it in the corporate colours of Enzed Fluid Connectors.

Stewart finished fifth overall on the 1985 Rally of New Zealand against world class opposition and then won both the Sight & Sound Rally and Hella Lights Rally in the national championship that year.

In 1986, Stewart crashed out of the Rally of New Zealand and did not drive the car in anger again, but later undertook a painstaking restoration back to full works specification and livery, wearing the rally plates and ID with which Blomqvist won the Acropolis Rally. The restoration was completed in 2005 and, since Stewart succumbed to degenerative motor neurone disease in 2009, the car has been on display in Oamaru as a tribute.

As with every true landmark in motor sport design and engineering, the Audi Quattro deserves the attention that is devoted to it by fans, collectors and competitors alike. It is testament to the brilliance of Audi, the vision of Ferdinand Piëch and his engineers and to the passion that motor sport, in its purest form, can engender.

'For me it was, of course, a fantastic period where you have a big competition but also a fantastic life,' said Michèle Mouton. Amen to that.

Appendices

Appendix 1 – Championships won

1982	FIA World Rally Championship for Makes
	German Rally Championship – *Harald Demuth/Arwed Fische, Audi Quattro*
	Swedish National Rally Championship – *Stig Blomqvist/Björn Cederberg, Audi Quattro*

1983	FIA World Rally Championship for Drivers – *Hannu Mikkola/Arne Hertz, Audi Quattro A1/A2*
	Rothmans British Open Rally Championship – *Stig Blomqvist/Björn Cederberg, Audi Quattro A1/A2*
	Austrian Rally Championship – *Franz Wittmann/Kurt Nestinger, Audi Quattro A1/A2*
	Finnish Rally Championship – *Lasse Lampi/Pentti Kuukkala, Audi Quattro A1/A2*
	SCCA North American Rally Championship – *John Buffum/Tom Grimshaw, Audi Quattro A1*
	South African Rally Championship – *Sarel van der Merwe/Franz Boschoff, Audi Quattro*

1984	FIA World Rally Championship for Makes
	FIA World Rally Championship for Drivers – *Stig Blomqvist/Björn Cederberg, Audi Quattro A2/Audi Sport quattro*
	FIA European Rally Championship – *Harald Demuth/Willy Lux, Audi Quattro A2*
	German Rally Championship – *Harald Demuth/Willy Lux, Audi Quattro A2*
	Austrian Rally Championship – *Franz Wittmann/Kurt Nestinger, Audi Quattro A2*
	Finnish Rally Championship – *Anteiro Laine/Risto Virtanen, Audi Quattro A2*
	SCCA North American Rally Championship – *John Buffum/Tom Grimshaw, Audi Quattro A1*
	South African Rally Championship – *Sarel van der Merwe/Franz Boschoff, Audi Quattro*
	Pikes Peak International Hill Climb (Open Rally) – *Michèle Mouton/Fabrizia Pons, Audi Sport quattro*

1985	Nordic Rally Challenge – *Per Eklund, Audi Quattro A2*
	Austrian Rally Championship – *Wilfried Wiedner, Audi Quattro A2*
	Finnish Rally Championship – *Anteiro Laine/Risto Virtanen, Audi Quattro A2*
	SCCA North American Rally Championship – *John Buffum/Tom Grimshaw, Audi Quattro A2*
	South African Rally Championship – *Sarel van der Merwe/Franz Boschoff, Audi Quattro A2*
	Pikes Peak International Hill Climb (Overall) – *Michèle Mouton, Audi Sport quattro*

1986	Austrian Rally Championship – *Wilfried Wiedner, Audi Quattro A2*
	Finnish Rally Championship – *Timo Heinonen, Audi Quattro A2*
	SCCA North American Rally Cup – *John Buffum, Audi Sport quattro*
	Cyprus Rally Championship – *Dimi Mauvropoulos, Audi Quattro A2*
	Czechoslovakian Rally Championship – *Leo Pavlik, Audi Quattro A2*
	Pikes Peak International Hill Climb (Overall) – *Bobby Unser, Audi Sport quattro S1*

1987	SCCA North American Rally Championship – *John Buffum, Audi Sport quattro*
	SCCA North American Rally Cup – *John Buffum, Audi Sport quattro*
	South African Rally Championship – *Geoff Mortimer, Audi Sport quattro*
	Pikes Peak International Hill Climb (Overall) – *Walter Röhrl, Audi Sport quattro S1*

| 1988 | South African Rally Championship – *Sarel van der Merwe, Audi Sport quattro S1* |

Appendix 2 – World Rally Championship victories

1981					
Rally	**No.**	**Crew**	**Car**	**Identity**	**Date**
Sweden	2	Mikkola/Hertz	Audi Quattro Group 4	IN-NV 90	13–15 Feb
Sanremo	14	Mouton/Pons	Audi Quattro Group 4	IN-NL 88	5–10 Oct
RAC	5	Mikkola/Hertz	Audi Quattro Group 4	IN-NM 61	22–25 Nov

1982					
Rally	**No.**	**Crew**	**Car**	**Identity**	**Date**
Sweden	4	Blomqvist/Cederberg	Audi Quattro Group 4	IN-DC 163	12–14 Feb
Portugal	7	Mouton/Pons	Audi Quattro Group 4	IN-NH 42	3–6 Mar
Acropolis	9	Mouton/Pons	Audi Quattro Group 4	IN-NU 40	31 May–3 Jun
Brazil	3	Mouton/Pons	Audi Quattro Group B	IN-NU 38	11–14 Aug
1,000 Lakes	3	Mikkola/Hertz	Audi Quattro Group B	IN-NN 82	27–29 Aug
Sanremo	9	Blomqvist/Cederberg	Audi Quattro Group B	IN-NK 54	3–8 Oct
RAC	1	Mikkola/Hertz	Audi Quattro Group B	IN-NU 84	21–25 Nov

1983					
Rally	**No.**	**Crew**	**Car**	**Identity**	**Date**
Sweden	3	Mikkola/Hertz	Audi Quattro A1	IN-NN 82	11–13 Feb
Portugal	3	Mikkola/Hertz	Audi Quattro A1	IN-NM 62	2–5 Mar
Argentina	2	Mikkola/Hertz	Audi Quattro A2	IN-NH 26	2–6 Aug
1,000 Lakes	1	Mikkola/Hertz	Audi Quattro A2	IN-NL-12	26–28 Aug
RAC	3	Blomqvist/Cederberg	Audi Quattro A2	44 CMN	19–23 Nov

1984					
Event	**No.**	**Crew**	**Car**	**Car**	**Date**
Monte Carlo	1	Röhrl/Geistdörfer	Audi Quattro A2	IN-NX 47	21–27 Jan
Sweden	1	Blomqvist/Cederberg	Audi Quattro A2	IN-NR 64	10–12 Feb
Portugal	1	Mikkola/Hertz	Audi Quattro A2	IN-NE 8	6–11 Mar
Acropolis	10	Blomqvist/Cederberg	Audi Quattro A2	IN-YD 29	26–31 May
New Zealand	3	Blomqvist/Cederberg	Audi Quattro A2	IN-NJ 5	23–26 Jun
Argentina	1	Blomqvist/Cederberg	Audi Quattro A2	IN-NC 59	27 Aug–1 Sept
Ivory Coast	1	Blomqvist/Cederberg	Audi Sport quattro	IN-NZ 9	31 Oct–3 Nov

1985					
Event	**No.**	**Crew**	**Car**	**Identity**	**Date**
Sanremo	5	Röhrl/Geistdörfer	Audi Sport quattro S1	IN-NM 7	29 Sept–4 Oct

Appendix 3 – European rally victories

1981					
Series	Rally	Crew	Car	Identity	Entrant
ERC	Jänner Rallye	Wittmann/Nestinger	Audi Quattro	IN-NV 90	Audi Sport
French	Terre de Garrigues	Mouton/Arii	Audi Quattro	IN-NP 60	Audi France/BP
ERC	Acosta Rally	Cinotto/Radaelli	Audi Quattro	IN-NL 77	Audi Italy/R6

1982					
Series	Rally	Crew	Car	Identity	Entrant
ERC	Jänner Rallye	Wittmann/Nestinger	Audi Quattro	IN-NL 88	Audi Sport
ERC	Hanki Rally	Blomqvist/Cederberg	Audi Quattro	NDC 163	Audi Sweden
German	Trifels Rally	Demuth/Fischer	Audi Quattro	IN-ND 37	Schmidt Motorsport
ERC	Costa Smeralda	Cinotto/Radaelli	Audi Quattro	IN-NP 40	Audi Italy/R6
ERC	Saarland Rally	Demuth/Fischer	Audi Quattro	IN-ND 37	Schmidt Motorsport
German	Metz Rallye	Demuth/Fischer	Audi Quattro	IN-ND 37	Audi Sport
Austrian	Pyhm-Eisenwurzen	Wittmann/Nestinger	Audi Quattro	IN-NL 88	Max Ogrisek
ERC	Scottish Rally	Mikkola/Hertz	Audi Quattro	LYV 4X	Audi UK
German	Voerderplatz-Rallye	Demuth/Fischer	Audi Quattro	IN-ND 37	Schmidt Motorsport
ERC	Hunsrüch-Rallye	Demuth/Fischer	Audi Quattro	IN-ND 37	Schmidt Motorsport
German	Esslingen-Rallye	Demuth/Fischer	Audi Quattro	IN-ND 37	Schmidt Motorsport
German	Sachs Baltic Rally	Demuth/Fischer	Audi Quattro	IN-ND 37	Schmidt Motorsport
Austrian	Semperit-Rallye	Wittmann/Nestinger	Audi Quattro	N451573	Schmidt Motorsport

1983					
Series	Rally	Crew	Car	Identity	Entrant
ERC	Jänner Rallye	Wittmann/Nestinger	Audi Quattro	N47.1573	Ogrisek/Funkberater
ERC	Arctic Rally	Lampi/Kuukkala	Audi Quattro	A-2053	Lampi/Shell
ERC	Boucles de Spa	Duez/Lux	Audi Quattro	IN-ND 37	Schmidt/Belga
ERC	Sachs Winter Rally	Demuth/Fischer	Audi Quattro	IN-ND 37	Schmidt Motorsport
ERC	Hanki Rally	Lampi/Kuukkala	Audi Quattro	A-2053	Lampi/Shell
Austrian	Lanvanttaler-Rallye	Wittmann/Nestinger	Audi Quattro	N47.1573	Ogrisek/Funkberater
Austrian	Arbö-Rallye	Wittmann/Nestinger	Audi Quattro	N47.1573	Ogrisek/Funkberater
Belgian	Haspengouw Rallye	Duez/Lux	Audi Quattro A1	N-RD 400	Schmidt/Belga
German	Metz Rallye	Mouton/Fischer	Audi Quattro A2	IN-NA 34	Schmidt/Votex
Austrian	Kufsteiner-Rallye	Wittmann/Nestinger	Audi Quattro	N47.1573	Ogrisek/Funkberater
Austrian	Pyhm-Eisenwurzen	Wittmann/Nestinger	Audi Quattro	IN-NL 88	Ogrisek/Funkberater
German	Esslingen-Rallye	Demuth/Fischer	Audi Quattro	IN-NA 4	Schmidt/Votex
Austrian	Admot-Rallye	Wittmann/Nestinger	Audi Quattro	N47.1573	Ogrisek/Funkberater
Austrian	Ennstal-Rallye	Wittmann/Nestinger	Audi Quattro	N47.1573	Ogrisek/Funkberater
Austrian	Semperit-Rallye	Wittmann/Nestinger	Audi Quattro	N47.1573	Ogrisek/Funkberater

1984					
Series	Rally	Crew	Car	Identity	Entrant
ERC	Jänner Rallye	Wittmann/Nestinger	Audi Quattro A2	IN-NM 65	Ogrisek/Funkberater
ERC	Arctic Rally	Laine/Kinnunen	Audi Quattro A2	U-4074	Laine
ERC	Costa Brava Rally	Cinotto/Radaelli	Audi Quattro A2	IN-NH 75	Audi Italia/SIV
Austrian	Wienerwald-Rallye	Wittmann/Nestinger	Audi Quattro A2	IN-NM 65	Ogrisek/Funkberater

1984 (continued)

Series	Rally	Crew	Car	Identity	Entrant
ERC	Harz-Winter-Rallye	Demuth/Lux	Audi Quattro A1	N-SM 250	Schmidt/Votex
ERC	Hanki Rally	Lampi/Kuukkala	Audi Quattro A2	A-2047	Sampo
French	Lyon-Charbonnières	Darniche/Mahé	Audi Quattro A2	7149RR75	Yacco
Austrian	Schneerosen-Rallye	Wittmann/Nestinger	Audi Quattro A2	IN-NM 65	Ogrisek/Funkberater
German	Trifels-Rallye	Demuth/Lux	Audi Quattro A1	N-SM 250	Schmidt/Votex
ERC	Saarland-Rallye	Demuth/Lux	Audi Quattro A1	N-SM 250	Schmidt/Votex
ERC	Arbö-Rallye	Wiedner/Zehetner	Audi Quattro	L29.888	MIG Linz
Austrian	Salzburg-Rallye	Wittmann/Nestinger	Audi Quattro A2	IN-NM 65	Ogrisek/Funkberater
Italian	Grand Sasso Rallye	Cinotto/Radaelli	Audi Quattro A2	IN-NH 75	Schmidt/SIV
German	Metz Rallye Stein	Demuth/Lux	Audi Quattro A1	N-SM 250	Schmidt/Votex
Turkish	Gunaydin Rally	Wurz/Geist	Audi Quattro A1	W 595393	Piz Buin
ERC	Scottish Rally	Mikkola/Hertz	Audi Quattro A1	MVV 44Y	Audi UK/Pirelli
Austrian	Pyhm-Eisenwurzen	Wiedner/Zehetner	Audi Quattro A2	IN-NM 65	Ogrisek/Funkberater
ERC	Barum Rally	Demuth/Lux	Audi Quattro A1	N-SM 250	Schmidt/Votex
German	Esslingen-Rallye	Demuth/Lux	Audi Quattro A1	N-SM 250	Schmidt/Votex
ERC	Škoda Rallye	Cinotto/Radaelli	Audi Quattro A2	IN-NH 75	Schmidt/SIV
German	Heidelberg-Rallye	Röhrl/Geistdörfer	Audi Sport quattro	IN-NC 64	Audi Sport
Austrian	Oststeirische-Rallye	Wittmann/Nestinger	Audi Quattro A2	IN-NM 65	Ogrisek/Funkberater
ERC	Hunsrück-Rallye	Demuth/Lux	Audi Quattro A1	N-SM 250	Schmidt/Votex
Austrian	Admont-Rallye	Wittmann/Nestinger	Audi Quattro A2	IN-NM 65	Ogrisek/Funkberater
German	Rallye-Deutschland	Mikkola/Herz	Audi Sport quattro	IN-NH 73	Audi Sport
ERC	Yu-Rallye	Wittmann/Pattermann	Audi Quattro A2	IN-NM 65	Ogrisek/Funkberater
ERC	Cyprus Rally	Buffum/Gallagher	Audi Quattro A2	WMN 44	Sutton/BF Goodrich
German	Baltic-Rallye	Demuth/Lux	Audi Quattro A1	N-SM 250	Schmidt/Votex
German	3-Städte-Rallye	Röhrl/Geistdörfer	Audi Sport quattro	IN-NH 73	Audi Sport

1985

Series	Rally	Crew	Car	Identity	Entrant
ERC	Jänner Rallye	Wiedner/Zehetner	Audi Quattro	IN-NL 1	MIG Linz, Moser
ERC	Arctic Rally	Laine/Virtanen	Audi Quattro A2	U-4074	Roadstar/Lokomo
ERC	Boucles de Spa	Waldegård/Thorzelius	Audi Quattro A2	N-SM 463	Schmidt/Belga
ERC	Harz-Winter-Rallye	Duez/Cantonati	Audi Quattro A1	IN-NL 1	Schmidt/Votex
Austrian	Schneerosen-Rallye	Wiedner/Zehetner	Audi Quattro	IN-NL 1	MIG Linz, Moser
ERC	Hanki Rally	Laine/Virtanen	Audi Quattro A2	U-4074	Auso Lasi
Greek	Kentavros Rally	'Jigger'/Stefanis	Audi Quattro A2		Avin
Austrian	Lavanttaler-Rallye	Wiedner/Zehetner	Audi Quattro	IN-NL 1	MIG Linz, Moser
Dutch	Tulip Rally	Bosch/Peeters	Audi Quattro A2	N-SM 210	Barron Audi
German	Metz Rallye Stein	Duez/Cantonati	Audi Quattro A2	N-SM 463	Schmidt/Votex
ERC	South Swedish Rally	Eklund/Whittock	Audi Quattro A2	HPK 987	Clarion
Austrian	Salzburg-Rallye	Wiedner/Zehetner	Audi Quattro	IN-NL 1	MIG Linz, Moser
Dutch	Achtmaal Rally	Bosch/Peeters	Audi Quattro A2	N-SM 210	Barron Audi
ERC	Scottish Rally	Wilson/Harris	Audi Quattro A1	MVV 44Y	MWM/Dunlop
ERC	Barum Rally	Demuth/Radaelli	Audi Quattro A2	IN-NN 17	Audi Italy/SIV
Greek	Biotia Rally	'Jigger'/Stefanis	Audi Quattro A2	IN-NH 75	Schmidt/SIV
ERC	Škoda Rallye	Demuth/Radaelli	Audi Quattro A2	IN-NN 17	Audi Italy/SIV
Greek	Black Rose Rally	'Jigger'/Stefanis	Audi Quattro A2		Avin
Austrian	Sprint Österreichring	Wiedner/Zehetner	Audi Quattro	IN-NL 1	MIG Linz, Moser
Austrian	Semperit-Rallye	Röhrl/Geistdörfer	Audi Sport quattro S1	IN-NY 18	HB Audi Sport

1986

Series	Rally	Crew	Car	Identity	Entrant
ERC	Arctic Rally	Laine/Virtanen	Audi Quattro A2	U-4089	Laine
ERC	Hanki Rally	Heinonen/Rindell	Audi Quattro A2	U-4600	Heinonen
Austrian	Schneerosen-Rallye	Wiedner/Zehetner	Audi Quattro A2	L 33 666	MIG Linz, Moser
Cyprus	Palm Trees Rally	Mavropoulos/Adams	Audi Quattro A2		Lord Jeans
Dutch	Amsterdam Rally	Bosch/Peeters	Audi Quattro A2	N-SM 210	Schmidt/Rothmans
Austrian	Lavanttaler-Rallye	Wiedner/Zehetner	Audi Quattro A2	L 33 666	MIG Linz, Moser
Cyprus	Tour of Cyprus	Mavropoulos/Adams	Audi Quattro A2		Lord Jeans
ERC	Arbö-Rallye	Wiedner/Zehetner	Audi Quattro A2	L 33 666	MIG Linz, Moser
Cyprus	Tiger Rally	Mavropoulos/Adams	Audi Quattro A2		Lord Jeans
Dutch	Ele Rally	Bosch/Peeters	Audi Quattro A2	N-SM 210	Schmidt/Rothmans
Austrian	Pyhm-Eisenwurzen	Wiedner/Zehetner	Audi Quattro A2	L 33 666	MIG Linz, Moser
Czech	Barum Rally	Pavlik/Jiratko	Audi Quattro A2	B 10-55	Team
Cyprus	Venus Rally	Mavropoulos/Adams	Audi Quattro A2		Lord Jeans
Austrian	Ring-Rallye	Wiedner/Zehetner	Audi Quattro A2	L 33 666	MIG Linz, Moser
Austrian	Vida Rally	Ferjancz/Tandari	Audi Quattro A2	IN-NH 75	Schmidt/Rothmans
Czech	Kosice Rally	Pavlik/Jiratko	Audi Quattro A2	B 10-55	Team
ERC	Hebros Rally	Ferjancz/Tandari	Audi Quattro A2	IN-NH 75	Schmidt/Rothmans
ERC	Cyprus Rally	Mavropoulos/Adams	Audi Quattro A2		Lord Jeans
Czech	Pribram-Rallye	Pavlik/Jiratko	Audi Quattro A2	D 10-59	Team
Greece	Black Rose Rally	'Jigger'/Stefanis	Audi Quattro A2		Avin
Cyprus	Tulip Rally	Mavropoulos/Adams	Audi Quattro A2		Lord Jeans
Austrian	Semperit-Rallye	Wiedner/Zehetner	Audi Quattro A2	L 33 666	MIG Linz, Moser
Dutch	West Kölm-Ahrweiler	Bosch/Peeters	Audi Quattro A2	44 NWN	Sutton/Yokohama

1987

Series	Rally	Crew	Car	Identity	Entrant
Dutch	Amsterdam BP Rally	Bosch/Peeters	Audi Quattro A2	N-SM 210	Schmidt/Yokohama
Dutch	Tulpen Rally	Bosch/Peeters	Audi Quattro A2	N-SM 210	Schmidt/Yokohama
Greek	Acheos Rally	'Jigger'/Stefanis	Audi Quattro A2		Avin
Greek	IFT Rally	'Jigger'/Stefanis	Audi Quattro A2		Avin
Greek	IFT Rally	'Jigger'/Stefanis	Audi Quattro A2		Avin

1988

Series	Rally	Crew	Car	Identity	Entrant
Cyprus	Palm Trees Rally	Mavropoulos/Antoniades	Audi Quattro A2		Shell
Cyprus	Tour of Cyprus	Mavropoulos/Antoniades	Audi Quattro A2		Shell
Cyprus	Tiger Rally	Mavropoulos/Antoniades	Audi Quattro A2		Shell

Appendix 4 – Scandinavian rally victories

1982					
Series	**Rally**	**Crew**	**Car**	**Identity**	**Entrant**
Swedish	Galve Rally	Blomqvist/Cederberg	Audi Quattro	NDC 163	Audi Sweden
Swedish	Halsinge Rally	Blomqvist/Cederberg	Audi Quattro	NDC 163	Audi Sweden
Swedish	Du Rally	Blomqvist/Cederberg	Audi Quattro	NDC 163	Audi Sweden
Swedish	South Swedish Rally	Blomqvist/Cederberg	Audi Quattro	NDC 163	Audi Sweden
Swedish	Kvastadansen Rally	Blomqvist/Cederberg	Audi Quattro	NDC 163	Audi Sweden
Swedish	Karlskronapokalen	Blomqvist/Cederberg	Audi Quattro	NDC 163	Audi Sweden
Finnish	Teboil-Rallye	Lampi/Kuukkala	Audi Quattro	LYV 5X	Lampi/Shell

1983					
Series	**Rally**	**Crew**	**Car**	**Identity**	**Entrant**
Finnish	Mesikammen Rally	Lampi/Kuukkala	Audi Quattro	A-2053	Lampi/Shell
Finnish	Pohjanmaan Rally	Lampi/Kuukkala	Audi Quattro	A-2053	Lampi/Shell
Finnish	Teboil Rally	Lampi/Kuukkala	Audi Quattro	A-2053	Lampi/Shell
Finnish	Teboil Rally	Lampi/Kuukkala	Audi Quattro	A-2053	Lampi/Shell

1984					
Series	**Rally**	**Crew**	**Car**	**Identity**	**Entrant**
Finnish	Manttä Rally	Laine/Kinnunen	Audi Quattro A2	U-4074	Laine
Finnish	Tampere Rally	Laine/Kinnunen	Audi Quattro A2	U-4074	Laine
Finnish	Teboil Rally	Lampi/Parala	Audi Quattro A1	A-2046	Lampi/Shell

1985					
Series	**Rally**	**Crew**	**Car**	**Identity**	**Entrant**
Finnish	Marcello Rally	Laine/Virtanen	Audi Quattro A2	U-4074	Laine
Finnish	Salpaussekla Rally	Laine/Kinnunen	Audi Quattro A2	U-4074	Roadstar-Lokomo
Finnish	Jyväskylän Winter Rally	Laine/Huolmann	Audi Quattro A2	U-4074	Laine
Finnish	Ita Rally	Laine/Huolmann	Audi Quattro A2	U-4074	Laine
Swedish	Masters Rally	Blomqvist	Audi Sport quattro S1	IN-NY 18	Audi Sport
Finnish	Lansirannikon Rally	Lampi/Kuukkala	Audi Quattro A2	A-2046	Lampi/Shell
Finnish	Teboil Rally	Laine/Huolmann	Audi Quattro A2	U-4074	Laine

1986					
Series	**Rally**	**Crew**	**Car**	**Identity**	**Entrant**
Finnish	Riimäki Rally	Laine/Eirtovaara	Audi Quattro A2	U-4089	Laine
Finnish	Malski Rally	Heinonen/Rindell	Audi Quattro A2	U-4600	Heinonen
Finnish	Salora Rally	Heinonen/Rindell	Audi Quattro A2	U-4600	Heinonen

Appendix 5 – British rally victories

1982

Series	Rally	Crew	Car	Identity	Entrant
Open	Mintex Rally	Mikkola/Hertz	Audi Quattro	LYV 4X	Audi UK/Pirelli
Open	Welsh Rally	Waldegård/Short	Audi Quattro	LYV 4X	Audi UK/Pirelli

1983

Series	Rally	Crew	Car	Identity	Entrant
Open	Mintex Rally	Blomqvist/Cederberg	Audi Quattro A1	MVV 44Y	Audi UK/BBS
National	York National Rally	Weidner/Hart	Audi Quattro	LYV 4X	Clearite
National	Granite City Rally	Weidner/Hart	Audi Quattro	LYV 4X	Clearite
Open	Welsh Rally	Blomqvist/Cederberg	Audi Quattro A1	MVV 44Y	Audi UK/BBS
Open	Scottish Rally	Blomqvist/Cederberg	Audi Quattro A1	MVV 44Y	Audi UK/BBS
Open	Ulster Rally	Blomqvist/Cederberg	Audi Quattro A1	MVV 44Y	Audi UK/BBS
National	Lindisfarne Rally	Weidner/Hart	Audi Quattro	LYV 4X	Clearite
National	Audi Sport National	Mouton/Barker	Audi Quattro A1	MVV 44Y	Audi UK/BBS

1984

Series	Rally	Crew	Car	Identity	Entrant
Open	National Breakdown	Mikkola/Hertz	Audi Quattro A1	MVV 44Y	Audi UK/Pirelli
Open	Welsh Rally	Mikkola/Hertz	Audi Quattro A1	MVV 44Y	Audi UK/Pirelli
Open	Ulster Rally	Röhrl/Geistdörfer	Audi Sport quattro	IN-NC 46	HB Audi Sport
National	Cumbria Rally	Wilson/Harris	Audi Quattro A1	MVV 44Y	MWM/Shell Oils
National	Audi Sport Rally	Wilson/Harris	Audi Quattro A1	MVV 44Y	MWM/Shell Oils

1985

Series	Rally	Crew	Car	Identity	Entrant
Open	National Breakdown	Wilson/Harris	Audi Quattro A1	MVV 44Y	MWM/Dunlop
National	Gwynedd Rally	Llewellyn/Short	Audi Quattro A2	44 CMN	Audi UK/Shell Oils

1986

Series	Rally	Crew	Car	Identity	Entrant
Open	National Breakdown	Mikkola/Hertz	Audi Sport quattro	44 WMN	Audi UK/Shell Oils
Open	Welsh Rally	Mikkola/Hertz	Audi Sport quattro	44 WMN	Audi UK/Shell Oils

Appendix 6 – Middle East rally victories

1987					
Series	Rally	Crew	Car	Identity	Entrant
Lebanon	Marlboro des Pistes	Saleh/Shahdoor	Audi Quattro A2		Rothmans

Appendix 7 – Pacific rally victories

1985					
Series	Rally	Crew	Car	Identity	Entrant
New Zealand	Sight & Sound	Stewart/Parkhill	Audi Quattro A2	MB 1440	Enzed
New Zealand	Hella Lights Rally	Stewart/Parkhill	Audi Quattro A2	MB 1440	Enzed

1986					
Series	Rally	Crew	Car	Identity	Entrant
New Zealand	Rally of the South	Stewart/Parkhill	Audi Quattro A2	MB 1440	Enzed

Appendix 8 – American rally victories

1982					
Series	Rally	Crew	Car	Identity	Entrant
SCCA	Norwester Rally	Buffum/Shepherd	Audi Quattro		Libra
SCCA	Olympus Rally	Buffum/Shepherd	Audi Quattro		Libra
SCCA	Northern Lights Rally	Buffum/Shepherd	Audi Quattro		Libra
SCCA	Susquehannock Trail	Buffum/Shepherd	Audi Quattro		Libra
SCCA	Budweiser Forest Rally	Buffum/Shepherd	Audi Quattro		Libra
SCCA	Miller Centennial Rally	Buffum/Shepherd	Audi Quattro		Libra
SCCA	Tour de Forest	Buffum/Shepherd	Audi Quattro		Libra
SCCA	Press on Regardless	Buffum/Shepherd	Audi Quattro		Libra
SCCA	Snowdrift Rally	Buffum/Shepherd	Audi Quattro		Libra

1983					
Series	Rally	Crew	Car	Identity	Entrant
SCCA	Acre Wood Rally	Buffum/Shepherd	Audi Quattro		Libra
SCCA	Budweiser Forest Rally	Buffum/Shepherd	Audi Quattro		Libra
SCCA	Norwester Rally	Buffum/Shepherd	Audi Quattro		Libra
SCCA	Michigan Rally	Buffum/Shepherd	Audi Quattro		Libra
SCCA	Susquehannock Trail	Buffum/Shepherd	Audi Quattro		Libra
SCCA	Molson Lobster Rally	Buffum/Shepherd	Audi Quattro		Libra
SCCA	Manistee Trail Rally	Buffum/Shepherd	Audi Quattro		Libra
SCCA	Press on Regardless	Mikkola/Pons	Audi Quattro		Libra
SCCA	Carson City Rally	Buffum/Shepherd	Audi Quattro		Libra

Appendix 8 – American Rally Victories (continued)

1984					
Series	**Rally**	**Crew**	**Car**	**Identity**	**Entrant**
SCCA	Norwester Rally	Buffum/Ward	Audi Quattro A1		Libra
SCCA	Michigan Rally	Buffum/Gallagher	Audi Quattro A1		Libra
SCCA	Susquehannock Trail	Buffum/Wilson	Audi Quattro A1		Libra
SCCA	Budweiser Forest Rally	Buffum/Wilson	Audi Quattro A1		Libra
SCCA	Oregon Trail	Buffum/Grimshaw	Audi Quattro A1		Libra
SCCA	Carson City Rally	Mikkola/Shepherd	Audi Sport quattro		Libra

1985					
Series	**Rally**	**Crew**	**Car**	**Identity**	**Entrant**
SCCA	Wild West Rally	Buffum/Grimshaw	Audi Quattro A1		Libra
SCCA	Olympus Rally	Mikkola/Hertz	Audi Sport quattro S1		Audi Sport
SCCA	Michigan Rally	Buffum/Grimshaw	Audi Quattro A1		Libra
SCCA	Budweiser Forest Rally	Buffum/Grimshaw	Audi Quattro A1		Libra
SCCA	Carson City Rally	Buffum/Grimshaw	Audi Quattro A1		Libra

1986					
Series	**Rally**	**Crew**	**Car**	**Identity**	**Entrant**
Canadian	Perce Neige Rally	Buffum/Grimshaw	Audi Sport quattro		Libra
NARC	Tulip 200 Forest	Buffum/Grimshaw	Audi Sport quattro		Libra
SCCA	Norwester Rally	Buffum/Grimshaw	Audi Sport quattro		Libra
NARC	Susquehannock Trail	Buffum/Grimshaw	Audi Sport quattro		Libra
SCCA	Arkansas Traveller Rally	Buffum/Grimshaw	Audi Sport quattro		Libra
SCCA	Ojibwe Rally	Buffum/Grimshaw	Audi Sport quattro		Libra
NARC	Dyfil St Agathe	Buffum/Grimshaw	Audi Sport quattro		Libra
SCCA	Press on Regardless	Buffum/Grimshaw	Audi Sport quattro		Libra

1987					
Series	**Rally**	**Crew**	**Car**	**Identity**	**Entrant**
SCCA	Barbary Coast Rally	Buffum/Grimshaw	Audi Sport quattro		Libra
SCCA	Centennial Rally	Buffum/Grimshaw	Audi Sport quattro		Libra
NARC	Susquehannock Trail	Buffum/Grimshaw	Audi Sport quattro		Libra
NARC	Sunriser Rally	Buffum/Grimshaw	Audi Sport quattro		Libra
NARC	Ojibwe Rally	Buffum/Grimshaw	Audi Sport quattro		Libra
SCCA	Press on Regardless	Buffum/Grimshaw	Audi Sport quattro		Libra
SCCA	Wild West Rally	Buffum/Grimshaw	Audi Sport quattro		Libra
Canadian	Tall Pines Rally	Buffum/Grimshaw	Audi Sport quattro		Libra

Appendix 9 – African rally victories

1983

Series	Rally	Crew	Car	Identity	Entrant
South African	Molyslip Rally	van der Merwe/Boschoff	Audi Quattro	CCN 70685	Audi ZA
South African	Tour de Valvoline	van der Merwe/Boschoff	Audi Quattro	CCN 70685	Audi ZA
South African	Mr X Faust Rally	van der Merwe/Boschoff	Audi Quattro	CCN 70685	Audi ZA
South African	Datsun International	van der Merwe/Boschoff	Audi Quattro	CCN 70685	Audi ZA
South African	Castrol Rally	van der Merwe/Boschoff	Audi Quattro	CCN 70685	Audi ZA
South African	Grensberg Rally	van der Merwe/Boschoff	Audi Quattro	CCN 70685	Audi ZA
South African	Jürgens Rally	van der Merwe/Boschoff	Audi Quattro	CCN 70685	Audi ZA
South African	VW Algoa Rally	van der Merwe/Boschoff	Audi Quattro	CCN 70685	Audi ZA
South African	Stannic Rally	van der Merwe/Boschoff	Audi Quattro	CCN 70685	Audi ZA

1984

Series	Rally	Crew	Car	Identity	Entrant
South African	Tour de Valvoline	van der Merwe/Boschoff	Audi Quattro	CCN 70685	Audi ZA
South African	Bosch Diesel Rally	van der Merwe/Boschoff	Audi Quattro	CCN 70685	Audi ZA
South African	Nissan International	van der Merwe/Boschoff	Audi Quattro	CCN 70685	Audi ZA
South African	Algoa Rally	van der Merwe/Boschoff	Audi Quattro	CCN 70685	Audi ZA
South African	Castrol Rally	van der Merwe/Boschoff	Audi Quattro	CCN 70685	Audi ZA
South African	Jürgens Rally	van der Merwe/Boschoff	Audi Quattro	CCN 70685	Audi ZA
South African	Stannic International	Demuth/Pegg	Audi Quattro	CCN 70685	Audi ZA

1985

Series	Rally	Crew	Car	Identity	Entrant
South African	Pretoria Brick 400	van der Merwe/Boschoff	Audi Quattro	CCN 70685	Audi ZA
South African	Wesbank Rally	van der Merwe/Boschoff	Audi Quattro A1	CCN 68012	Audi ZA
South African	Castrol Rally	van der Merwe/Boschoff	Audi Quattro A1	CCN 68012	Audi ZA
South African	VW Algoabaal Rally	van der Merwe/Boschoff	Audi Quattro A1	CCN 68012	Audi ZA
South African	Border Mountain	Mortimer/Pegg	Audi Quattro A2		Audi ZA
South African	Stannic International	van der Merwe/Boschoff	Audi Quattro A1	CCN 68012	Audi ZA
South African	Tour de Valvoline	van der Merwe/Boschoff	Audi Quattro A1	CCN 68012	Audi ZA

1986

Series	Rally	Crew	Car	Identity	Entrant
South African	Sam 400	van der Merwe/Boschoff	Audi Quattro A1	CCN 68012	Audi ZA
South African	Castrol Rally	van der Merwe/Boschoff	Audi Quattro A1	CCN 68012	Audi ZA
South African	Valvoline Rally	van der Merwe/Boschoff	Audi Quattro A1	CCN 68012	Audi ZA
South African	Stannicberg Rally	Mortimer/Woodhead	Audi Quattro A2		Audi ZA
South African	Tolken Toyota Rally	Mortimer/Woodhead	Audi Quattro A2		Audi ZA
South African	VW Algobaal Rally	Mortimer/Woodhead	Audi Quattro A2		Audi ZA

1987					
Series	**Rally**	**Crew**	**Car**	**Identity**	**Entrant**
South African	Tour de Valvoline	Mortimer/Boschoff	Audi Sport quattro	CCN 68012	VW ZA
South African	Wesbank Rally	Mortimer/Boschoff	Audi Sport quattro	CCN 68012	VW ZA
South African	Castrol Rally	Mortimer/Boschoff	Audi Sport quattro	CCN 68012	VW ZA
South African	VW Algoa Rally	Mortimer/Boschoff	Audi Sport quattro	CCN 68012	VW ZA
South African	Stannic Mountain Trial	Mortimer/Boschoff	Audi Sport quattro	CCN 68012	VW ZA
South African	Toyota Dealers Rally	Mortimer/Boschoff	Audi Sport quattro	CCN 68012	VW ZA
Zimbabwe	Monomatapa Rally	Rautenbach/Holm	Audi Quattro	CCN 70685	
Zambia	Zambia Rally	Rautenbach/Archenoul	Audi Quattro	CCN 70685	

1988					
Series	**Rally**	**Crew**	**Car**	**Identity**	**Entrant**
South African	Nissan Rally	van der Merwe/Boschoff	Audi Sport quattro S1	CCN 70686	VW ZA
South African	Wesbank Rally	van der Merwe/Boschoff	Audi Sport quattro S1	CCN 70686	VW ZA
South African	Castrol Rally	van der Merwe/Boschoff	Audi Sport quattro S1	CCN 70686	VW ZA
South African	Stannic Rally	van der Merwe/Boschoff	Audi Sport quattro S1	CCN 70686	VW ZA

1990					
Series	**Rally**	**Crew**	**Car**	**Identity**	**Entrant**
Zimbabwe	Zimbabwe Rally	Rautenbach/Mitchell	Audi Quattro	CCN 70685	
Zimbabwe	Cresta Rally	Rautenbach/Mitchell	Audi Quattro	CCN 70685	

1991					
Series	**Rally**	**Crew**	**Car**	**Identity**	**Entrant**
Zimbabwe	Cresta Mutoto Rally	Rautenbach/Mitchell	Audi Quattro	CCN 70685	

Appendix 10 – Enthusiasts' directory

Where to Buy a Quattro

Bonhams
101 New Bond Street, London, W1S 1SR
Tel: +44 20 7447 7447
Fax: +44 207 447 7401
Email: info@bonhams.com
www.bonhams.com

Mark Donaldson Ltd.
The Granary, 1 Waverley Lane, Farnham, Surrey, GU9 8BB
Tel: +44 (0) 1252 759009
Email: info@markdonaldson.com
www.markdonaldson.com

Where to Prepare a Quattro

AM Cars Quattro Specialist
Station Road, Ilminster, Somerset, TA19 9BL
Tel: +44 (0) 1460 55001
Fax: +44(0) 1460 55566
Email: amcars@amcarsquattro.co.uk
www.amcarsquattro.co.uk

Pro-Tec Performance
Unit 6, Clifton Business Park, Preston New Road, Clifton, Lancashire, PR4 0XQ
Tel: 01772 633777
Email: protecmotorsport@btconnect.com
www.pro-tecmotorsport.com

Where to Visit a Quattro

Audi Tradition
Auto Union GmbH, 85045 Ingolstadt, Germany
Tel: +49 7132 311345
http://trshop.audi.de

National Motor Museum
John Montagu Building, Beaulieu, Brockenhurst, SO42 7ZN
Tel: 01590 612345
www.beaulieu.co.uk

Where to Rally, Volunteer or Spectate with Quattros

Eifel Rallye Festival
John Davenport (UK)
Email: john.davenport@eifel-rallye-festival.de or
       sebastian.klein@eifel-rallye-festival.de
www.eifel-rallye-festival.de

Goodwood Festival of Speed
www.goodwood.com/motorsport/festival-of-speed

Race Retro (UK)
Tel: +44 (0)207 384 8175
Email: lee.masters@clarionevents.com
www.raceretro.com

Rallying With Group B (UK)
Tel: 07973 380411
Email: rwgb@live.co.uk
www.rallyingwithgroupb.net

Slowly Sideways (UK)
Email: Tim.Bendle@slowlysidewaysuk.com
www.slowlysidewaysuk.com